BECOMING MOLLY-MAE

BECOMING
MOLLY-MAE

BECOMING MOLLY-MAE

MOLLY-MAE HAGUE

EBURY
SPOTLIGHT

1

Ebury Spotlight, an imprint of Ebury Publishing
20 Vauxhall Bridge Road
London SW1V 2SA

Ebury Spotlight is part of the Penguin Random House group
of companies whose addresses can be found at
global.penguinrandomhouse.com

First published by Ebury Spotlight in 2022

www.penguin.co.uk

A CIP catalogue record for this book is available from the British Library

ISBN 9781529148770

Printed and bound in Great Britain by Clays Ltd, Elcograf S.p.A.
Imported into the EEA by Penguin Random House Ireland, Morrison
Chambers, 32 Nassau Street, Dublin D02 YH68.

Penguin Random House is committed to a sustainable future
for our business, our readers and our planet. This book is
made from Forest Stewardship Council® certified paper.

To my family. Mum, Dad and Zoe x

CONTENTS

GROWING UP FAST

STEPPING INTO THE SPOTLIGHT

LOVE AND FRIENDSHIP

FACING THE TRUTH

PRACTISING SELF-CARE

INTRODUCTION

AN EXTRAORDINARY LIFE

Growing up, I always used to say to my mum that it scared me – the idea of not making the most of my life. I remember having this conversation with her so many times: I'd tell her how I was fearful of just growing old, sitting in my rocking chair and regretting that I'd not done more. I wanted to be able to look back and tell my grandkids, 'I did things that were completely out of the ordinary. I did crazy, big things.'

Now, don't get me wrong, now that I'm older, I know just how there is nothing at all wrong with an 'ordinary' life – I know a lot of people would love a life that could be called that! And in many ways it's the everyday parts of my life – the times when I'm at home, curled up on the sofa in front of a film – that make me the happiest today. But, looking back, that was my way of expressing as a kid that I wanted to live a life that *I* wanted – that I wanted to create my own path.

And that desire has shaped so many of my choices. For better or worse, I have always been drawn to doing the unexpected thing: whether that was entering pageants, going to fashion school in London, even having my lips done at a young age (more on how I feel about *that* later) and, last but not least, starting to build a career on social media. I've always felt that impulse to do more, achieve more, experience more. I never wanted to do just what other people expected for me – and now I'm living a life I still can't believe. But what you see online can only tell half the story …

In this book, for the first time, I want to share it all with you, revealing the highs, lows and everything in between, online and off. From getting my start on social media and becoming an influencer, to finding myself on *that* island, building a business empire and juggling work and love, all in the glare of the spotlight. I'll tell you what's really gone on, how I've felt and the lessons I've learned – and am still learning!

At 23, I'm definitely a work in progress, and I want to share with you all I've gone through in my life up to this point. I'll reveal the things that I've dealt with along the way, from my friendships and body-image worries to relationship stress and online trolls. And I'll show you just how I've managed to get myself back in balance each time, work hard and create a life I love – categorically.

I want this book to make you laugh, make you think, make you feel inspired and, most of all, make you realise that you too can achieve your dreams.

FIRST STEPS

A LITTLE GIRL
WITH BIG DREAMS

My parents always say that the way I look at life doesn't come from them. My mum used to joke, 'Molly's not ours, she's the milkman's child!' because it just wasn't really normal in my family to have all this ambition, to have these big dreams … but then there was my auntie Jackie.

I often say that a lot of my ambition came from my auntie Jackie – that's my dad's sister. She really was someone who I truly looked up to when I was growing up. She had an incredible job. She drove an incredible car (a Porsche). She had an incredible house. She was always draped in Louis Vuitton bags and designer clothes – my mum says that I definitely got my love for the nicer things in life from my auntie! And she was always seeing really successful guys. Plus, she was just beautiful, with long blonde hair; she really looked after herself.

But the fancy clothes and bags and cars weren't the reasons I admired Jackie. I looked up to her because she taught me that you could do it for yourself: Jackie was an accountant, which is what gave her this great lifestyle. When I looked at my auntie, I knew: *That's the life I want to live. I want to be like her when I'm older. I want to have money of my own. I want to be an independent, strong woman.*

Even as a child, I just knew that whatever I ended up doing, it needed to be big and out of the ordinary. And though they might not necessarily want all the same things from life as I do, my family has always been so understanding and supportive of that. They've let me be myself – and supported in me in so many ways – which I'm so grateful for. As you'll see, they really helped me get started, first as an influencer, and later as I grew my businesses.

But to start, let's go back a bit earlier ...

FAMILY TIME

I was born in 1999 in Stevenage, Hertfordshire, at Lister Hospital, with a distinctive strawberry birthmark on my forehead (and no, I don't have it anymore). I grew up in Hitchin, another town in Hertfordshire, and lived in the same house almost all my childhood with my mum, Deborah; dad, Stephen; and sister, Zoe, who's three years older than me. My parents met working in the police. They've both had long careers with the Hertfordshire police force: my mum started as a police officer, then worked in the control room answering 999 calls, while my dad ended up as an inspector before retiring from the police. I've always loved telling people they were police officers and am super proud that those were their jobs.

My family is so small: no cousins, only one living grandparent – just tiny. Both my grandparents on my dad's side died when I was really young, while my mother's dad died when she was only 24. When I talk on Instagram about how small our family is, my dad will sometimes message me, reminding me, 'Molly, you have lots of cousins twice removed that follow you on here!' But to me, my family is the people who were there on Christmas Day and on birthdays: my mum, dad and sister, my nana (my mum's mum) and my auntie Jackie. (And since they remember these early years better than me, I'll let them tell you a bit about what I was like, too.)

When I think back to my childhood, I always think about the holidays we had as a family. We never went to Disneyland or Florida or anything like that for our holidays – we'd go to the Isle of Man for a walking trip, hiking every day, or something like that. My parents would take me and my sister to climb ridiculously big mountains like Snowdon in Wales and Helvellyn in the Lake District! We were such an active family.

Our sporty lifestyle was mostly driven by my dad. He's always kept fit and is actually an ultramarathon runner these days, so it makes sense that he pushed me and Zoe to get into sports and be healthy. He was always taking the two of us swimming or running, and if there was adrenalin involved, he'd jump in feet first. When we'd go on a family outing to a theme park or water park, for instance, he'd be the one taking us round on all the rides. I think he loved them as much as we did! So in that way he was just a big kid and a really cool dad to grow up with.

While my mum was active too, she's the one who encouraged my creative, theatrical side. Raising us girls, she was just the most dedicated, caring mum. She wanted the best for us and really inspired me to go for my dreams. Not only that, but she went to great lengths to help me make them happen. From when I was young and showed a desire to perform onstage, she'd drive me to theatre auditions all over the country. One year, a theatre group we knew about was putting on a production of *Annie*, and I really wanted to get the lead role. Like I said, she took me all over the place to audition for it, and I know that even if I'd got the part at a theatre three hours away, she'd have been there, taking me to every rehearsal – she was that invested. (Sadly I was never cast for anything but the chorus! But more on that later ...)

On Sundays we used to go to church, because my nana is really religious, and we'd have a roast dinner, but that wasn't really our special family time. The happy family time that I remember having together would be on those walking holidays: going to the Lake District, going to Wales, walking round the Isle of Man – that was sort of how we bonded as a family.

My friends would be on summer holidays to America or Egypt, and I'd be in waterproof trousers and a rain mac, walking 12 miles a day at eight years old. I walked up Snowdon at six, which just goes to show the way my parents were: there was no opting out of things like that. (Looking back, I think my mum would have probably wanted to go to Florida as well! But my dad loved those active holidays, so we'd do it for him.)

KEEPING BUSY

We weren't just an active family on holidays, either. I was put into every single extracurricular activity possible. First it was ballet and Brownies, when I was younger. Later on, I swam five times a week, ran twice a week, played an instrument (the cello), had singing lessons, was in the local youth orchestra and the choir, did Irish dancing ... you name it. If there was a club, I was in it.

Molly's mum, Deborah: *'As a child, Molly was strong-willed, adorable, beautiful, entertaining, funny, and loved putting on little shows – she loved the stage, but was never picked for the main roles (only ever the chorus), which was always a source of frustration for her. She was self-driven and won a competition for a teen magazine photo shoot at about age 11, which she entered herself. She knew her own mind, even if that meant getting her gorgeous long hair cut off in preference for a Frankie from The Saturdays look.'* (Which I will tell you about later!)

'She was a talented cellist – she was never going to play an instrument that any of the other children in her class played.

But she was her swimming coach's worst nightmare … She hated swimming and put little effort into her training. As a result he often had her out on the side doing press-ups as punishment!

'As Molly got older, she and I had an amazing bond. She would never want to go on sleepovers and always wanted to be at home. When she went on a school ski trip, she was terribly homesick. But she was very confident: later on, when she started with Insta, she knew exactly what look she wanted. Sometimes she'd reject hundreds of photos!

'How would I describe her these days? She is unargumentative and generous. She loves her family and friends deeply. She is charitable and always gives to the homeless, just the same as when she was a child and would give up a bar of chocolate for someone living on the street. She's very humane and sensitive (she would never watch the film Marley & Me, *as it's about the death of a dog). And she hates blood and needles (yet loves a horror film). Her bad habit now is only being in contact when she has a problem. I guess that's what mums are for!*

'In the future, I would love to see her in a presenting role on TV. I would like her to use her platform to be a good role model for young women. I would like her to be financially secure for life. Most of all, I want her to be healthy and happy and have a long life.'

As I've said, my parents were really sporty – both marathon runners. Zoe, too, is very talented at sport, but that was more her thing than mine. These days, Zoe's a medic and a PT in the army, so she basically trains the other army members to be fit. Whatever I did, I tried to do it to the best of my ability. (OK, maybe not so much with the swimming! But I didn't really get that sporty gene.)

In almost every activity I did, there was an element of competition. From the swimming to the running to the Irish dancing, there was always that scrutiny. Still, I was never actually that good at anything that I did then, but I was fine with that. It didn't bother me whatsoever.

At one point, the swimming coach actually suggested to my dad not to bring me anymore. He told him, 'She's not any good. She's actually holding the rest of the squad up – we're having to not carry on to the next 100-metre freestyle, because she's still finishing that 100-metre backstroke. She can't do it!'

But my dad told him, 'She's doing it and she will get better at it.' Even if I'd never be a champion swimmer, I was learning a real lesson in perseverance: how to commit to something without expecting an immediate reward.

Molly's dad, Stephen: 'Molly was a difficult baby in terms of lots of projectile vomiting, which bounced off the wardrobe doors in her bedroom like a scene from The Exorcist.' (Thanks, Dad!) 'She was a light sleeper, too: I used to have *to lie on the floor next to her cot and have a hand on her back through the bars, then crawl out of the room when she finally slept – then she would wake the minute I was over the threshold, so I spent a lot of time sat in the rocking chair in her room with her.*

'As a kid she was delightful and energetic and fun from the off – I used to love my time with her when I was on rest days from the police and Zoe was at nursery or school. I would take Molly to the local pub, where they had a large soft-play area, and we would play and draw and colour for hours – such great fun. I also used to take her to a large shopping centre with designer clothes shops from a young age as it was a safe space for her to wander and had lots to see. So maybe it's my fault she got into some things! We'd go there with my mum and have a walk and a cake and spend time just watching the world.

'As dad to two daughters, I felt it was unfair for a girl to have the birthmark in such a prominent location – I used to get into verbal fights with people who said rude things about it when they saw it and only because I was a copper did I stop myself "chinning" a few. Once she started school, she was a cheeky monkey: teachers either loved her or didn't – at a young age it was 90 per cent who loved her, and the birthmark gave her an adorable quality. A lot of people stood up for her and protected her from cruel remarks – I genuinely think this birthmark defined some of her resilience to the media that she has now.

'As a youngster, Molly was always looking for her passion. Eventually, she found herself in terms of Irish dancing and some stage acting and singing at school. I would absolutely love taking her to full-weekend Irish feis (competitions) and often was the only dad there doing his daughter's hair or helping the mums do the food. Again, it was such fun and I loved cheering her on.

'Molly joined her sister at swimming and spent many hours at swim training, but I remember she was just there for the social time and chats with mates. Now, I can see it was her character: she is and always has been a people person. Other parents loved her; teachers and instructors found her frustrating as she knew her own mind and stood her ground – great qualities I watched develop in her and now see as strong parts of her being. She would always argue with me, but from a fact-based point, and she'd often win. I'd then find myself resorting to "I'm your dad, do as I say."

'She was always too scared to go on school trips and stay away from home or sleep over at friends' places. She would go and then come running back in the late hours. At the same time, she was always outgoing. She and Zoe would sing, dance and play together so well on camping trips and keep each other entertained – they would make fun of me constantly, as I had no rhythm or timing and couldn't dance. They would often say, "Dad, keep the beat to this," as we were driving, and they knew I had no chance!'

For me, my favourite thing of all was Irish dancing. I was danc-ing from a young age, six or seven, and I really, really loved that. It wasn't something that ran in our family: it was just that, one evening at the pub, a friend of my mum's had mentioned that she was taking her daughter to this Irish dancing class. My mum thought, *Oh, I'll send Molly with her, then* – and that was it. Soon, I was dancing three times a week. No one at school was doing Irish dancing; it was seen as a really different hobby to have. But again, it was that thing of my always wanting to be doing some-thing a bit different.

My parents would take me to all the *feis* competitions and it could get expensive as well, to buy all the kit: we needed special dresses, shoes and even wigs. In Irish dancing, you wear wigs made up of loads of ringlets so that when you jump, the ringlets bounce up to give the illusion that you're jumping higher, to impress the judges. One of these wigs would cost maybe £100, which felt like so much money to spend on a wig at that age. When my auntie Jackie bought me one for my birthday, I just thought it was the best thing I'd ever been given. It was completely the wrong colour for me, because I had quite mousy brown hair then, and this wig was bright blonde. I didn't care! I loved a bit of glam, even then.

Despite the glam, it was hard work: it's crazy, the commitment that goes into Irish dancing. I did it for quite a few years, eventually placing fourth in the All England competition when I was about 14. I wouldn't say I was ever really *that* good at it, but I did love it. It was just so fun.

Auntie Jackie: *'Growing up, Molly was fantastic to be with: fun, laughing, always giggling – her personality shone through from an early age. I have to say she loved clothes and dressing up, and had a real passion for her appearance, which is no surprise when we look at where she is today. She was constantly changing outfits, and you could also see that when she was doing her Irish dancing, she absolutely adored this and getting into costume. I remember when she was about six, I bought her a beautiful Irish dancing wig, which she took great pleasure in wearing.*

'She was fun, loving, caring, but very focused. I think she struggled to find her real passion in her early to mid-teens – but then when she did find it, she absolutely blossomed and really found out what she wanted to do with her life. Today, clearly, she's very busy, and very driven, but she's got a clear vision for her future. And she's learning all the time, and has had to learn incredibly quickly since she came out of Love Island, *which I think she struggled with at the start. But now, she's got a good team around her and she's doing incredibly well.*

'The best things about Molly? Her vision, her drive, her artistic nature and how hard she works to achieve her goals. The worst things? That's really tricky. I would say probably one of her weaknesses, which hopefully she'd agree with, is the fact she doesn't like conflict or having disagreements with people – that will come with experience and knowing how to handle things. But I think we can also say that when she feels that she's right,

she will absolutely argue her corner. I would also say that she has a weakness for expensive things, but she probably got that from me at an early age. So I'm not going to worry ... or take any blame for that whatsoever!

'In the future, I see only good things: happiness and health – those will bring her all the rewards that she wants. And I see her increasing her profile, not just on social media but in the wider world as well. With hopefully some exciting new ventures that she's got coming up ...'

WHAT I'VE LEARNED
FROM MY PARENTS

Schoolwork, of course, took up a lot of time, too. My parents always wanted me and Zoe to achieve great things and be high-performing kids in everything we did. They weren't the sort of parents that would ever let us get away with not doing our homework. I had after-school tutors for subjects that I wasn't really doing well in. And if I ever got detention at school, I would be absolutely petrified to tell my dad because I really respected my parents, and my sister and I just never wanted to upset them. I never wanted to let them down – especially my dad, as he had really high expectations.

Between school and all our activities, Zoe and I were kept really busy. My parents' friends would sometimes tell them, 'You need to let the girls have some time off!' If I wanted to go to a friend's house for tea, I usually wouldn't be able to because I'd have three after-school clubs that day. I'd have already been swimming and running before I even got to my Irish dancing class at eight in the evening. Zoe was just as busy, and – though we were very different – we got on very well, and still do.

Molly's sister, Zoe: *'The main thing that stands out for me about growing up with Molly is how different we were but how well we got along. Molly always liked the finer things in life – loved to be up to date with the latest fashion trends. She was incredibly outgoing; there was never silence or a dull moment. Even going to family dos or meeting people for the first time, I'd always leave Molly to do the talking because she can just waffle so well!*

'At school I remember being so proud of her and wanting everyone to know she was my sister. She loved acting and singing, and in my eyes had such potential. But teachers never really seemed to like her (I think because she was so loud and confident), so she always just got the parts in the chorus.

'Molly to me now is the most generous sister ever, always offering to pay for things, buy me things. Still liking the finer things in life but also appreciating you don't have to spend a fortune to look nice. When anyone ever asks me about her, I always describe her as someone with their head screwed on and

who knows, business-wise, what she wants. I believe she's done so well in her job because she knows what is going to make her succeed in life. There was a number of times at the start of coming out of Love Island when Molly's manager, Fran, would ask her if she wanted to work with certain companies, and Molly would give her a straight "NO!"

'I know now that Molly will always be at the other end of the phone for me, and vice versa. I've always said she'll be the only person I can ever really trust, and I know she feels the same way about me. We'll always have a bond that I'll be forever grateful for, and I'm glad that she'll always be my best friend.

'Saying all this, sometimes Molly is so busy, I struggle to get ahold of her. But honestly that's the only negative I have to say – oh, and that she doesn't let me borrow her nice clothes! But other than that I can't fault her. Molly has a very exciting future ahead of her. I can tell this is only the start. She and Fran, working together, will have some great ideas planned. I know Molly is excited to have a family with Tommy one day, although I always tell her not to rush! I'm very excited to be a part of Molly's future and can't wait to see what she has in store for herself.'

My parents were happy as long as I was busy with my activities and focusing on my schoolwork. But they could be strict. Growing up, I wasn't allowed to even go into shops that were a bit more expensive or label-y when I was with my mum. She didn't really bring me up to be interested in all that (but of course I drifted in that direction anyway, because of my auntie!). Mum is just so not materialistic. She's not into anything designer – loves to shop in charity shops. My parents also made me learn all my times tables before I could get my ears pierced. I was 10 when I finally got them done!

I remember specifically an argument we had a few years later, when I was 14 and all my girlfriends were going to get their acrylic nails put on for the summer … I was just not allowed. My dad's position was, 'There's just not a chance. You're too young.' I was crying for three days because all I wanted were these acrylic nails that all my friends were getting. But that's how strict my parents were, even with little things like that. They really didn't want me to grow up too quickly. At school, I was known as the police officer's daughter, and I think my dad's job – both my parents' jobs, being in the police, but my dad was the stricter one – did impact the way they brought us up.

When my friends started drinking at parties, from the get-go I knew I wasn't going to, because if my dad found out, it just wouldn't have been worth it. I wouldn't even have tried to get away with that! I did, however, get a bit more freedom as I got older, especially if I was with Zoe – they trusted her to look after me. I actually went to my first club with Zoe. We managed to get into a pool bar called Osinsky's, which turned into a club as the night went on. It was the place where everybody in Hitchin went on the weekend. Zoe was very protective of me – she was like another mum to me back then (she wouldn't let me drink alcohol that night!) – and it was a really fun night. But I knew what the boundaries were, and I wasn't going to do anything wild or that I felt would have let my parents down.

I really wouldn't change the way they raised me, as much as it could be annoying. For instance, when I turned 14, their attitude was, 'If you want to go into town with your friends, you need to go get a job and start working to earn your money – we're not going to give you money for that.' And it was exciting for me at that age, the thought of having my own money and being able to buy my own things. I really wanted to get a job so I could go into town with my friends and buy clothes. A lot of my friends were getting jobs, too, doing paper rounds and other things. I knew I didn't want to do a paper round – working somewhere like a hairdresser seemed much more up my street.

So, I wrote a CV, and I went round town with my dad. I really was so nervous at first. I even made him go into one hairdresser and hand in my CV as I stood outside. But the receptionist told him, 'If it's for her, then she needs to come and hand in the CV herself!' So, I did – and by the end of the day, I'd handed my CV to what felt like every single hairdresser in Hertfordshire to try to get a job. In the end, I got a good job at a salon, working there all day every Saturday and after school on Thursdays. The manager was really scary, so it was petrifying at times, but overall I was quite happy getting paid five pounds an hour to just sweep the floor, make tea and wash hair (which I was never very good at).

I'm glad my parents helped me to build a strong work ethic from a young age. So yes, they pushed me in every aspect of my life. And I think I'll raise my kids, when it happens for me in the future, the exact same way, because I think my upbringing and their values – the importance of hard work, of doing the right thing and of achieving your absolute best – really did shape me in terms of becoming who I am now.

FINDING
MY FUTURE SELF

Growing up, I had all sorts of hopes and dreams. We always thought Zoe was going to be a police officer, because that's the field our parents both worked in and she took a massive interest in that. But I don't think we really knew what I was going to do. My grades at school were fine: As, Bs and Cs – I was a middling student. (I hated maths and science and wasn't great at them, while I got an A star in drama.) I just remember my parents wanting me to be academic and work really hard in school and get an amazing job.

I think if you'd said to my parents when I was growing up, 'Do you want your child to go on Love Island *when she's older?' they'd have said no – put it that way!*

For a while, I really wanted to perform. Acting, singing, dancing – I just wanted to do everything! I was in a couple of West End shows when I was around 15 – small productions – as well as some more local ones. I signed up with an agency that put me forward for jobs, and my mum would take me to so many auditions as I really, really wanted to get into that world. My parents really would have done anything to help me achieve my dreams and do whatever I wanted at that time, be that going into the theatre or whatever else it was. They'd do the best they could to help me get there.

On one level, theatre suited me: I've always been loud and confident, so going into an audition wouldn't scare me. It's just the way I'm wired. Whenever I look back at my life, I never remember a stage of being even a tiny bit shy – I've just always been an extrovert. But I always ended up getting chorus roles and never the big parts I wanted. I think my theatre dreams died a natural death over time, and, looking back, I'm kind of glad they did. That's a route that I could have definitely tried to go down more seriously, but it's such a hard path; some of the friends I made in those circles are still trying to make it now, and you have to be the best of the best to do so in that industry. I knew I wasn't there. I knew I wasn't a good-enough singer or a good-enough dancer to make it. So, I had yet to find a path that was right for me …

GETTING INSPIRED

In the meantime, I was getting into social media. My sister gave me her old iPod Touch when she got her first iPhone, and I downloaded the Instagram app on that. I still remember the old layout – it was just so simplified. There was no Stories feature then, and you could only upload one picture per post; you couldn't post multiple photos for followers to swipe through.

But it's changed a lot in the years that I've used it. I've always loved Instagram, from such a young age, and always enjoyed using the app – not just to post to but to scroll through. I didn't really use Twitter at the time, and I never had a Facebook account at all even though all my friends were on it. For me, it was all about Instagram.

Why? It's multiple things. For one thing, I'm quite a nosy person, so I've always enjoyed looking at other people's lives! You get a bit of an insight into what people are up to. I follow accounts where people post every day, so you can really see what they are wearing, doing and saying day-to-day. Trends change so much, so it's nice to be able to look down at your Instagram feed and see what's happening. And, honestly, it actually can be educational as well! Sometimes I'll find out things that are in the news via Instagram. I think it's just a really good place to stay up to date, so you always know what's going on.

And obviously now, with Instagram Stories, people post what they're doing throughout the day, and it's more unfiltered. I put a lot of things on my Stories that I wouldn't post on my main feed, and I think that people are interested in them because they love to know the ins and outs of your life, from what coffee you're getting at Starbucks to what foundation you're using. People really, really like to know those things – me included! So, I love watching other people's Stories and can find myself scrolling for hours – it's a bit of an escape from my own life (not that I've really ever tried to escape my life, but it's still fun to dip into someone else's).

Back then, when I was starting out, I really looked up to a lot of Australian influencers, like Tammy Hembrow. I followed travel influencers, too, because I wanted to travel the world, but Emily Shak was my main inspiration – she was *the* girl. Every picture she posted was in a different location. She was always doing something different. I loved it all: how unique her posts were, how classy she was. She always had amazing make-up and hair, and everything about her screamed that she was the influencer.

I still think that now. She just knows what she's doing and she's very good at her job. She's got this effortless quality – although now I realise all the work that goes into that. Years ago, I'd be looking at Emily, thinking, *God, how is she this effortless?* I didn't realise until I was doing it myself what actually goes into getting to that stage. She was probably driving for hours to go to that location to get that cool picture, like I do!

Later, through work, we became good friends. Now it makes me laugh that I was fangirling over her – I was obsessed! But an influencer's job is literally to influence people, so if I wasn't feeling influenced by Emily, then she wasn't doing our job correctly. Because she was so good at her job, I was just obsessed with everything she did. And when you're starting out on Instagram or YouTube – or, really, in any other field that you want to get into – having people that you look up to, and want to be doing the same things as, really helps develop your love for it.

Soon I was obsessed with watching YouTube as well. On there, it was Patricia Bright who I really looked up to – and who I still admire. She's just everything: she's hilarious, she's business-savvy, she's accessible, she has cool style. She has a real loyal following of subscribers and now has a more finance-focused YouTube channel, too, where she makes videos about how she budgets and so on. She just radiates that 'business boss bitch' vibe, and I really wanted to be like her. Later, I got to work with her on a YouTube video we filmed together, which, like getting to know Emily, was another moment that felt like life was really coming full circle. Imagine 15-year-old me knowing Patricia had asked me to come on her channel?

> *In terms of Instagram, Emily Shak was the OG for me, and then YouTube, it was Patricia Bright. They were my main two girls.*

Feeling inspired, I started uploading my own photos on Instagram: selfies, photos I took in the mirror of my outfits, pictures of my hair (I often put it in a fishtail braid at the time, so I'd be taking pictures of that). Showing different hairstyles was something that was easy for me to do – I didn't need to spend money to style my hair in a nice way – and people followed me for my hair content from quite early on. I always wanted to travel the world but I didn't quite have the money to do that yet, so my Instagram was predominantly fashion (which is funny, really, because some of my outfits were absolutely shocking back then!). But if you look at my Instagram then and look at it now, you can definitely see the consistency from the very beginning, in terms of how I use it and what I've been interested in. It wasn't as if I thought, *I know, I can make money from influencing. Let's try that.* It was a really organic move because it was my passion.

Soon, I was growing on it: I had around 8,000 followers by the time I was about 16. People at school would ask, 'How on earth do you have 8,000 followers?' And I didn't really know – it just happened so quickly for me. Part of it was that the timing was right: I started out just before Instagram became really popular, so I'm lucky that I caught it then, when not as many people were posting the way I was posting. But most of all, I just loved using the app, and I took it seriously from the start. A lot of my friends used to ask me to give them shout-outs on my Instagram account, and I always used to say no! Even back then, I cared how I was coming across on social media, and what my Instagram looked like, and I took a lot of pride in that.

I always say, if there's one thing I know my stuff about, it's definitely Instagram! I know the app inside out. I know what works on there, and I know what doesn't.

It is a bit of a mad feeling when I think today there are girls that look at me in the same way I looked at Emily, Patricia and other influencers. Say, if I go to Manchester, it blows my mind how many people will come up to me and ask for pictures – and I take it as a total compliment. It's a surreal feeling: girls actually follow me and know who I am. I can't believe that now I'm that girl! And I love the idea of girls being inspired by me in turn.

Zoe: '*Throughout our childhood I remember lots of laughter, always making up silly songs and dance routines – Molly getting her first digital camera at a young age and already making silly vlogging videos with us arguing in the background.*

'*I have a vivid memory of Molly returning from a day out with her best friend Molly Hughes and her showing me some pictures they took (she must've been about 12 years old), posing behind trees, and me thinking how pretty she looked and how photogenic she was. I think it was this moment when something clicked in her, and from then on she was always dressing to impress – which we disagreed on a lot!*'

(Molly: Growing up, Zoe and I just didn't see eye to eye over what I wore. I was going in the completely opposite direction to what she'd probably expected, as we were super different. I would wear high-heeled stiletto boots just to go into town, and she'd look me up and down, clearly thinking, *What is she doing?!* With Zoe being the older sister, I think she was coming from a protective point of view – she didn't want me growing up too fast. I think it was when I moved out that she sort of realised that I wasn't a child anymore. I could pay my rent, I could pay my own bills and she couldn't mother me, if that makes sense. Now, we're totally accepting of our differences.)

'As she grew up, obviously the pictures and videos became a lot more serious. I'd always have to be taking Insta pics and I'd be absolutely mortified when people would watch us. We used to bicker a lot when it came to getting the right shot – which would sometimes take up to an hour, even with 10,000 followers – all worth it in the end! She's always had such a good eye for finding the right location and always knew exactly what she wanted.'

DEALING WITH DIVORCE

Not everything was smooth sailing growing up. Back then, my biggest fear was always that my parents would get a divorce. I think that's quite a normal thing for kids to be worried about. I believed that I'd be OK as long as my parents didn't split up. And I was always so scared of that. But looking back, maybe the situation at home was playing a part in those fears: my mum and dad didn't really get on and would often argue.

On a Saturday, I'd come back from orchestra practice and the first thing I'd say to Mum would be 'Have you had an argument with

Dad while I've been gone?' Because if they had, it could literally last all weekend and the atmosphere would just be awful. At home, we would all just be on top of each other, feeling bad energy, bad vibes.

And it was quite a predominant theme of my childhood – my parents not getting on. I think that's why I do and I don't like Christmas now; for me, it brings back a lot of sad memories, as it was always a time when there would be friction. Later on, after they'd split up, I realised, *Oh, this is why Christmas has always been the way it has.*

When I was about 14 or 15, they sat down and told me together that they were getting a divorce. They told me that they were splitting up because they just didn't love each other anymore and no longer wanted to be together. I felt heartbroken. I couldn't believe that my greatest fear had come true – my parents were actually getting a divorce. But it also made me understand why things were the way they were when I was growing up: why they'd never kissed or cuddled. Looking back, I think it was always obvious that my parents weren't really happy together.

After my parents split up, my dad moved out to a new flat, and the house in Hitchin where I'd grown up was sold. My mum bought a new-build house in Langford, a nearby village, but it was still under construction, so we actually lived in a log cabin on a campsite for about six months, waiting for it to be built. There's still one picture on my Instagram feed where, if you look really closely, you can see the wooden slats of the log cabin!

The period after my parents split was really, really hard. Because she'd been in relationships all her adult life, my mum was playing catch-up in terms of what she'd missed out on. She'd been engaged to a guy when she was 18, and when they broke up, she met my dad straight away. So, now she was on all these dating websites, doing her thing, going out.

And in that first year after the divorce, Mum really struggled. For a very short while just after the divorce, she turned to alcohol to cope with the pain of the breakdown of their marriage, which sort of explains why I am the way I am with alcohol – I pretty much avoid it. I associate those difficult times after my parents' divorce with alcohol being involved and my mum drinking too much – understandably, because her marriage had broken down. But I felt like I had to look after my mum for a while; it was kind of a role reversal, where she was the child.

Zoe had turned 18 by this point and had gone travelling for a year. The aftermath of the divorce wasn't why she went, but she did get to escape the situation at home, in a way. I don't think she realised what I was left to deal with, because she left when things were OK. But I do remember one night when it all came to a bit of a head: Zoe was away in Thailand or somewhere equally far-flung, and my mum had a guy round at our house and I felt really upset about it. I was texting my sister, saying, 'I hate Mum, I can't do this anymore, I'm so upset.'

What I didn't realise was that I was sending those messages to my family group chat with my mum and my dad (my parents had stayed amicable after the split). It was really bad; I was saying some awful things. I actually didn't care so much that my dad was going to see them, but I didn't want to let my mum know how I felt. But afterwards, Mum came to find me and gave me a massive hug, saying, 'I'm really sorry you feel like this.'

And, in time, things did calm down and we all got a lot more settled in our new situation. These days, my mum and I have a super close relationship and are so open with each other – almost friends, as well as mum and daughter. But I do know what that specific night taught me: always quadruple-check where you send your messages – because it will never leave me, that feeling when I knew I'd sent those messages in the family group!

. . .

Now, I think of the divorce as a terrible time where I had to grow up fast, but I don't think I found it particularly agonising. I get a lot of questions on my Instagram these days from girls messaging me, asking, 'How did you get through your parents' divorce? I'm going through it now.' My attitude was *This is just something I've got to go through – it is what it is.*

> *There was nothing that I could say or do to make it better, I just had to go through it. Sometimes, with tough times, you do just have to make it to the other side.*

It does help to find a good friend to lean on. My best friend growing up was a girl called Molly Hughes; her mum was my mum's best friend, and Molly's parents went through a separation at the exact same time as mine. Molly and I were *so* close, practically sisters, and we really helped each other through this rough patch in both our lives. I'm so grateful I had her and I hope I was as much a support for her as she was for me. Besides that, it's hard to give advice because everyone's so different – and I know for some people, a divorce can just feel like the worst thing in the world.

What I will say, though, is that sometimes something as painful as a divorce can actually lead to better things. My mum, especially, has completely changed in my eyes following my parents' split. When she was still with my dad, she very much took a backseat to him. Maybe because he was always taking charge of things, and doing things with us that she was too scared to do, she just seemed a lot more timid and meek. Nowadays, I get to see her as this strong, independent woman, and I can see that she's actually so much more laidback and chill than I thought. When it came to my prom after-party, she agreed to have it at her house, even though it meant having all these kids over! She listens to the same music as me and Zoe and is just so fun and relaxed. I don't know if I would've got to see this side of her if she and my dad had stayed together.

Another bonus is that both my parents have moved on to new relationships with partners that they're really happy with: my dad's now married to Carla, who he met through the police, while my mum met her partner, Jon, on a dating site, and they recently got married too, in the summer of 2021. So, it really can all work out for the best.

GROWING
UP FAST

SPREADING
MY WINGS

The minute my parents got a divorce was a turning point for me, in terms of going from a girl to more of a woman, even if I was yet to turn 18. I became a lot more independent, doing my own thing and getting a boyfriend. While my parents were together, I could never really bring a boy home. It was very different when my parents divorced; once my dad moved out, I had much more freedom to do what I wanted. Before that, I couldn't get away with anything!

That's not to say anything went with my mum. She's a massive worrier – a real panicker – and I think that was probably due to her job with the police: she'd hear these horror stories every day, and it's hard to not imagine them happening in your own life. But her big thing was just knowing where I was at all times, and then I was alright to do what I wanted.

Still, I didn't do anything too wild. I was more focused on what I could do next ...

LIFE LESSONS AT FASHION SCHOOL

In the same way that I was always doing something different to what my friends were doing – never really wanting to do the same after-school clubs as them, for instance, but instead getting into Irish dancing – I didn't really want to do the same things as them after our GCSEs. I don't mind admitting that I've always wanted to be that person that people would think of and say, 'Oh, did you see that Molly-Mae went and did that? Did you see that she went and did this?'

Some people might not like the sound of that. They might not like being spoken about, and they might not think it's something you should seek out – but we're all different! I actually think that my attitude of always striving for more has led me to where I am today. My motivation to succeed comes from always wanting to be doing something bigger and better and to exceed people's expectations of me. Even now, I want to be making moves that have people thinking, *I can't believe she's doing that at that age!* When I was younger, it was just the same – and my decision to go to fashion school was an example of that.

My friends were staying on at our school, the Priory School, for sixth form. And I didn't want to do that because I thought, *I don't want to be like everyone else. I don't want to stay on and do A levels. I'd only be doing that because everybody else is doing it.* And that's not the way I live my life.

I knew I loved fashion, so I found something that appealed to me far more than the idea of sixth form. I applied for the Fashion Retail Academy in London, went for an interview – my dad came with me, bless him – and I got in. That was a massive thing for me, and surprised some of the people around me: 'Oh my God, where are you going – to fashion school in London?' It was so cool, so different, and I loved that!

Of course, other's people's reactions to something like that and the reality of doing it are not quite the same thing … I actually ended up almost quitting fashion school at the start, after just a couple of days.

What prompted that was that I'd had this knot-in-your-stomach feeling where I felt sick and shaky and on edge – what I'd call anxiety. I've had it at times throughout my life, like when I went to sleepovers as a kid (and, as my dad mentioned, would want to come home!), and the whole week before my driving test – things like that. When I had to perform in front of people, I'd just get general nerves, which weren't so bad – but I reckon if I'd got to the level that I actually wanted to with performing, rather than being in the chorus, I probably would have had that anxious feeling then, too.

And I definitely had it as I started fashion school.

I thought, *I've done the wrong thing in coming here.* I felt really out of my depth. Looking back, I was scared. So, I actually decided to go back to my old school for sixth form, to see if that would be a better option for me. Thinking I would stay on for A levels after all, I picked out business, drama and music – but I didn't study in my spare time, so on some level I knew it wasn't gonna work! And it wasn't what I really wanted to do. But I was also thinking, *Oh God, I can't do fashion school. I don't have the confidence.* Part of me just wanted to stay in my comfort zone.

But back at school, everyone was doing the same thing, still in the same groups – it was all very much the same. I realised, *Actually, I don't want to stay here anymore, this is just boring to me.* I thought, *No, I'm going to do this, I'm going to stick to my guns – I'm going to fashion school!*

And I did, I went back to fashion school the very next day. The anxiety did linger for a little bit, but I just told myself, 'You've tried sixth form and it's not for you. This has to work.' And, after a week or so, I was fine – I made friends and felt much more settled. I spent two years there in the end and got a level-three qualification in fashion retail. The course covered buying, merchandising, window dressing – it was very broad. But because of my passion for fashion, it came naturally to me. I had to be in college in London two days a week, so I was able to work at home and earn money, too.

Looking back, it was the best thing I ever did, taking a risk to go there. I made some really good friends and have some really good memories. Fashion school also opened horizons for me: I was travelling into London twice a week on the train, then going all over the city, and that really helped me get very streetwise and taught me a lot about being independent. I was meeting new people, networking, doing things that I would never have done if I'd stayed where I was.

When I look back and think about how I was trying to tread a different path to everybody else, my decision to go to fashion school was definitely key to that.

But I don't regret that one day I went back to my old school, either. I needed to have that moment of realising that nothing's going to change if you stay in the same situation. And I needed to learn that feeling uncomfortable doesn't have to mean you've made the wrong decision. With a lot of things that I do, I can still go through waves of anxiety and really overthink even my day-to-day choices: *Oh God, am I making the right decision?* But it's totally normal to feel nerves – especially when you're doing new things, but even in your everyday life, too.

You should never feel guilty about that – it's very normal to second-guess yourself – but remember: it doesn't mean you've done the wrong thing. Sometimes, you need to get out of your comfort zone to get to where you want to go!

FINDING MY STYLE

Every day I went to FRA, I would try to put together a nice outfit because obviously it was fashion school, and everyone was judging you on what you were wearing! So, I think I learned a lot about fashion then and what suited me.

Essentially, my style is simple and casual. I'm never really dressed up, unless I'm going to an event or absolutely have to be. Day-to-day, it's tracksuits, trench coats, leather jackets; I love leggings with a jumper, a nice long coat and a trainer or boot. I'm very rarely wearing jeans – if I am, it will be very baggy mum-style jeans, so that they're nice and comfy. Because I hate uncomfy clothes. I just like my outfits to be very wearable, chilled, not OTT. I didn't have any money when I was at fashion school and finding my look, and even today other girls can recreate my outfits really easily, because they're nothing too crazy – mostly high-street in terms of budget, mixed up with some designer items.

And I do put my outfits together myself, at least when it comes to my own content. For shoots with Beauty Works and Pretty Little Thing, I regularly work with the same stylists, who know the kinds of clothes I like to wear and bring options they think I'll like. But most of the outfits that you see on my Instagram are what I've put together, depending on what mood I'm in: sometimes I just want to be casual and sometimes a bit more dressy (relatively!).

On days that I'm struggling to put together an outfit, I love using Pinterest for inspiration. I'll just have a look around, then look in my own wardrobe and see what I've got, to try to find something a bit different to what I've done on my feed recently. For instance, if I've worn black in the most recent picture, I'll make sure I'm not wearing black again. But I don't try to follow the trends on Instagram; I just wear what I want to wear, when I want to wear it.

And my style does change regularly. I used to love, love, love wearing high-heeled boots everywhere I went, because I was self-conscious about my legs. I did a shoe haul video a few years ago, and it was all heels. Even when I was just going into town with my mum, I'd be in high heels. Now, I just don't feel that way. I'm almost always in trainers.

Ultimately, my fashion philosophy is this: wear whatever the hell you want to wear – don't try to follow what everyone else is wearing. And if you get it 'wrong'? When I look back on my Instagram, I still sometimes think, *Oh, why did I wear that?* Or, *What I was I thinking that day?!* Everybody gets it 'wrong' sometimes – but it probably felt good at the time, so who cares? Fashion should be something to have fun with it, rather than worrying if you've got it 'right'.

MY PAGEANT YEARS

Studying in London wasn't the only way my world was opening up during that time. I know that every single activity I did when I was younger, my parents encouraged me to do in the hope that one of those might become my career (you never know, maybe I'd end up a cellist!).

But as I got older, I was becoming more self-aware and realising I could make my own choices. I didn't actually have to do every single thing my parents said. One day, I put my foot down over swimming. I just said to my dad, 'I'm not going anymore – I don't want to go!' My parents had spent so many hours taking me to these activities and paying for all these things; for your child to then say they actually don't want to do all that anymore, I bet it's quite heart-wrenching. But it was a part of my growing up. I was starting to understand what I was really interested in, and what really appealed to me … and it wasn't swimming club.

What I'd enjoyed most about the Irish dancing *feis* – competitions – had always been the dressing up, and doing the make-up, the fake tan, the hair. So, when I was contacted about competing in a pageant here in the UK, I thought, *This is great – like a* feis, *but without having to do the painful dancing!* (And yes, it could be painful when you worked at it.) The pageant scene wasn't really that popular in Britain – it was more of an American thing – but I thought, *I want to try that!*

So, I did. I The pageant was just an online process at the start. I ended up getting through that initial round to represent my area, making me Miss Teen Hertfordshire. That meant my mum had to take me to the finals in Blackpool, where I competed in my first pageant at age 16 for the Miss Teen Great Britain title – quite a big one.

I didn't have the first clue what I was doing. I had no idea that you're meant to present a folder in your interview with the judges, where you explain about all the charity work you've done – I hadn't known about the folder or the charity work, so I didn't do very well that year. The interview was a massive part of the pageant: in terms of scoring, about 50 per cent related to the stage element (what people typically think of when they hear the word 'pageant', where you're walking in front of an audience in your beautiful dress) and 50 per cent hinged on the interview.

Still, I placed in the top 16 that first year. Afterwards, I said to my mum, 'Next year, I'm coming back and I'm gonna win it – I really, really want to do this.' Finally, my competitive side was coming out! The funny thing is, I wasn't competitive in anything before pageants because with my other activities – swimming, running and so on – I knew I was never going to win. But suddenly I felt I *could* win this – this was something that I could actually be good at. I could talk a good interview. I could walk well onstage. I could do my hair and make-up really nicely. I could actually do well … and so, for the first time, I really had that hungry desire to actually win something.

And I really set my mind to it. There's a lot more that goes into pageants than people might know: I raised thousands and thousands of pounds for charity (I did everything, but mostly a lot of cake sales!). I've always felt a sense of achievement doing charity work and have always been a charitable person, so being able to give back as part of my pageant work was something I loved to do.

I also made appearances as my county representative; as Miss Teen Hertfordshire, I'd go to car boot sales, church gatherings, all over the place. Unlike what a lot of people may think, winning a pageant isn't really about what you look like – it's more about the things you do in the prep for it, showing that you give back to your community.

So, I went back the next year and, now that I knew what I had to do to prepare, I was crowned one of the winners: I won the title of World Teen Supermodel UK 2016/17 – a mouthful!

• • •

After that, I ended up travelling to China to compete in the international round that followed. I spent two weeks over there competing. It was scary; I'd never been anywhere like that before. I hadn't been anywhere much further than France! But it was an amazing experience. The pageant was held in a place called Macau, which is famous for its hotels and gambling, a bit like a Chinese Las Vegas. I didn't get to see a lot of it – really only what I saw getting a taxi from the airport to the hotel – as we literally spent two weeks inside its downstairs reception room, rehearsing every morning, afternoon and night. I spent my eighteenth birthday out there, rehearsing for this pageant! I actually did quite well and placed second, so I was first runner-up.

I didn't do any more pageants after that as I got busier with other things, but I am so glad that I had the experience. The stereotype around pageants is that the girls taking part aren't very nice to each other, but I made some really good friends through that world, including my friend Misha, who's actually an influencer herself. I know it sounds cringey, but you do make friends for life when do you do something like that, because everyone has the same interests as you. They want to be the girl in their area that's doing something a bit different. They want to be onstage, they want to be in the spotlight.

For another girl, it may not be pageants that appeal to them. It might be football, or painting, or camping – anything! But you will meet like-minded people if you get involved with what interests you.

Pageants also really let me explore my love for make-up and hair – and all the glitz and glam that comes with being onstage.

I'm such a girly girl and always have been, and pageants really let me indulge that side of me.

They gave me (even!) more confidence, too, as I was putting myself out there, going for what I wanted and seeing my hard work pay off.

These days, I look back on all the rejections I had when I was younger and see every 'no' as almost paving the way for each 'yes' that was to come: all those auditions where I didn't get the role; all the school plays where I went for the main part and I was never chosen. I've said to my mum, sometimes I feel like all that rejection that I had when I was younger – never being the one chosen to do the things I wanted to do, or who was the best at everything – is why I'm so appreciative of the life I have now. I've realised that it just wasn't my time then, and I feel so lucky to be where I am today. I really do believe that a negative situation can lead to something positive. When something bad happens, you never know if there could be something positive around the corner.

So, after never really achieving what I wanted to achieve, I think, now, maybe that's because I needed to go through all that to then get this.

MY WORLD OPENS UP

Instagram was, of course, another major focus for me then. At fashion school, I always dressed up for my two days a week – it was *fashion* school! – and then, on our lunch breaks, I'd ask my friends to take pictures of me in crazy outfits on the streets of London. They were terrible, terrible pictures, looking back – but I was living my London fashion student dream. That's really when I started to grow on that platform, because I was always trying to post what I was doing on my socials. I guess it was to reiterate, 'I'm out here doing this really cool thing!' I always wanted to show everyone that I was up to something interesting – it was, again, that impulse to be different. So, I really began posting, posting, posting, as much as I could, and trying to save as much money as possible so I could buy more clothes and style them for outfits for Instagram shoots.

And it wasn't just Instagram keeping me busy, either. At 17, I made my first video for YouTube. Sat in the dining room at about eleven o'clock at night, I made a tutorial on how to wave your hair with straighteners. I thought, *I'm just going to film it and put it up,* and then I posted about it on my Instagram, saying, 'Go watch my first video.' It wasn't my best video. I filmed it on a camera that I'd saved up to buy, but it wasn't expensive equipment. But with anything like that, you have to start somewhere and just keep posting as much as you can.

I was working as a lifeguard at the time, alongside going to fashion college. When I went into work the next day, everyone was talking about the video I'd made – because no one we knew really did that at that point; no one made YouTube videos. But me being me, I wanted to be original.

After that video, I started filming once a week. I'd use my mum's debit card to place a big order from PrettyLittleThing or another brand to film a haul video, and promise her that I was going to send it all back once I'd talked through the clothes I was buying. Occasionally, I'd forget to return the order in time. That *was* a bit naughty. But I didn't have any money, so I couldn't afford to do hauls otherwise, which were so popular at the time; they were blowing channels up. I kept thinking, *If* I *get a haul that blows up, it'll be worth it …*

In the end, what eventually got me quite a few subscribers was uploading a hair tutorial on how I did my bouncy pin curls for pageants; in it, I explained how I would cool them and set them. That got about 150,000 views, which was a huge amount then. It's always the case that one video will blow up a channel and then that's it: people will just keep coming back to your channel and you're on your way.

*I didn't know that video was going to go big
– you never do! You just have to persevere
and hope that one video will take off.*

And I really wanted that to happen, for this to become some-thing more than a hobby for me. Those hauls aside (sorry, Mum!), I always wanted to have my own money and to be able to buy things for myself – to, say, be able to go and buy a top I wanted. From following other girls on Instagram and YouTube, I knew social media meant I could turn myself into a business, and that's what I wanted to do. My entrepreneurial streak was coming out.

So, unlike how I got started on Instagram, with YouTube, it was always *This could be a job!* It wasn't a case of *I want to do this video just because I really enjoy it.* I did enjoy it. I loved it! And I actually still do love it! Even now, with my workload, I still edit my videos myself because I find it really therapeutic. I don't let anyone else do it, and I do really relish that aspect.

*I knew YouTube could be a job.
I didn't do it just because I thought
it was a bit of fun. I thought,
Something could come from this.*

But I was very aware from the get-go that YouTube could be some-thing that could make me money, that could be a job for me. And that's totally fine to think that way – it's fine to think about how you want to make a living. It's a *good* thing to put some thought into what you want to do! And, in my case, I was beginning to feel like being a successful influencer could actually be the answer to everything I'd always wanted. To be my own boss, to make good money, to have fashion, hair, beauty and make-up all be part of my job? That'd be incredible.

Because I wasn't that keen to make any of my other jobs my career …

BAD JOBS AND
GOOD INTENTIONS

In the swimming club I swam with, when you hit 17, you became a lifeguard – that's just what you did. So, the minute I turned 17, I did my lifeguard course and became a lifeguard, just as my sister had. I was so happy to be getting paid £8 an hour as it helped me to save up.

It wasn't a fun job whatsoever. You literally sit on a chair most of the time, just watching the swimmers. There was only one time I had to do something: a boy was choking in the outdoor swimming pool and I had to give him a few backslaps – that was literally it!

So, it was a quiet job, but it still came with a lot of responsibility. They used to tell us that if someone drowned on our watch, it could be taken really seriously – so it was quite a serious job to have as a 17-year-old. These days, my manager, Fran, and the girls

I work with have a long-running joke about me being proud of being a lifeguard, because for a while, every time I was asked in an interview to share something people didn't know about me, I'd mention that! Even now, if ever I'm on a boat and it gets a bit bumpy, I'll tell people not to worry: I'm a lifeguard! I'm joking, but it *is* something I'm proud of. I guess it's quite an interesting thing to say you can save someone's life and do CPR.

So, on the days that I wasn't at fashion college, I was lifeguarding in my first year. In my second year, I started working at Boots instead, on the No7 make-up counter. That was just a Christmas temp job at first, then they wanted to take me on; fashion school was Mondays and Thursdays, so I'd work at Boots on the three days in the week I wasn't at college. It was a good job, but I didn't love it. For anyone who hasn't worked in retail or customer service, let me tell you, it can be tough! Some people can be quite rude. But I have the gift of the gab, as my mum says, which definitely came in handy at times.

• • •

With my two years at fashion school up in the summer of 2017, I left Boots to try something different: working at a gym. I wanted to do so many different things when I was younger and, for a while, I thought I wanted to be a personal trainer. At the time, I was really into spinning classes, so I started working at the gym on the desk as a receptionist. I also started learning how to become a spin instructor. It was almost a mini-apprenticeship, so I'd be leading classes myself. I was learning on the job, with the aim of potentially making that my actual career. But from doing all that I definitely lost my love for exercise for a while. My shift would start at 6am, so I'd be up at 5am to get ready, then I'd walk to the gym. Once there, I'd turn on the lights, switch on all the machines and do my shift. By the time it was over, I wouldn't want to stay any longer to do my own workout because I'd had enough of the machines!

I kind of got fired from the gym in the end. Basically, I had glandular fever, and I was just so, so unwell that I was signed off from work by a doctor for a month. Towards the end of that time, I started to feel a bit better, but I thought, *I'll go back to work when I'm 100 per cent recovered.* In the meantime, I had to take part in a ceremony to hand back my pageant crown. I went to get my hair done for that and was spotted at the hairdresser's by one of the gym members, who then told the gym staff.

The other thing was, I'd left my email account open on the gym computer (don't do this!), and my manager saw an email receipt that showed I'd gotten an Uber in London at about 3am. I'd been on a night out with my college friends and was coming all the way home after missing the last train! At the time, we were going through a stage when, every other weekend, we'd go to a different club in London – DSTRKT, Libertine, Tape – and try to get in. We made some really fun memories, actually. I'd never do that now, but I was at that experimental age, and my fashion college friends were quite into that kind of stuff. I'd catch the last train home if it wasn't too late, or I'd stay in London at a friend's house, or we'd all split a hotel room and share a double bed.

Of course, that all got me into trouble at the gym. My manager asked me, 'You've had all the time off work, Molly. Are you really unwell?' I had been! But I probably should have gone back to work a bit earlier. It was quite a small team, and I think they'd struggled without me there, so they were quite upset with me. They called me in for a disciplinary meeting and had all this evidence to show that I wasn't unwell. After that, my dad helped me write a long resignation letter, accepting responsibility for my actions. He probably took it more seriously than me at the time because it was an area that he worked on in the police and obviously anything Zoe or I did reflected back on him. But it did help me to learn that accepting responsibility for things is super important.

Looking back, all those jobs helped me to learn what I *didn't* want from a job. I realised that I get bored very easily, which is why I couldn't stay in a job for long. I was chopping and changing all the time because they just weren't for me. And that really reinforced for me what I'd always known: I wanted to do something a bit different to what was on offer to me – I just didn't know what yet.

That's why what I'm doing now is so incredible to me.

MAKING
MONEY MOVES

After I got semi-fired from the gym, I went to Ibiza to work the season, at the start of summer 2018. We have this joke in my family that I'm never home for my birthday, I'm always in a different country, doing something different with a different set of people. For my eighteenth I'd been in Macau for the pageant; now, for my nineteenth birthday, I'd be in Ibiza, working at a beach club as a door girl. The club was *the* place to work on the island. I interviewed for the job in London and loads of girls went for it, so I was really excited to get it.

And the job itself was OK. When people walked in, I'd be on reception, asking, 'Would you like to book a table?' and walking them to it. The minimum spend for a table was £500, and with that you'd get unlimited food and drinks … but I really wasn't enjoying it. I was so homesick and hardly made any friends. A lot of people around me were taking drugs. Before a shift, I'd go into someone's bedroom at 10am, and they'd be sniffing drugs on their dressing table. I just thought, *I can't be around this. My parents are in the police! They did not raise me to be OK with being around this stuff.* I stayed about two weeks and went home.

But what may have seemed like a mistake at the time actually led me further down the path I truly wanted to follow …

NO LOOKING BACK

The one good thing about that experience was that, even in the short time I was in Ibiza, my Insta following went up quite a bit – people liked the fact that I was posting from this new place – and I hit around 16,000 followers while I was there. I was also getting on the radar of brands. In the run-up to my trip, I'd already been tagging brands in my posts when I wore their clothes, so they'd notice me. That meant that, before I went to Ibiza, my absolute favourite, PrettyLittleThing, sent me some clothes that I packed to shoot. And a brand from Instagram also gifted me some outfits for my trip; I remember they paid me £70 to upload three posts featuring those outfits while I was there. I could not believe that a fashion company wanted to pay me to take pictures in their clothes and post them on Instagram. I thought, *This is happening!*

By this point, I was desperate to become a full-time influencer. I was sure this was what I needed to do, that this was my calling. It incorporated everything I loved – hair, make-up, fashion – with everything I wanted to do, including being my own boss. So, I was determined not to get another job when I got back from Ibiza. I told my dad, 'Look, I'm making money! Give me this year to let me do influencing, and I'll make this work. I've had other jobs and I don't want to do that anymore. I want to try to make Instagram my career.'

It was important to me that my parents were OK with my decision, so that's why I asked my dad, even though technically I was old enough to do whatever I wanted. Yes, I'd become a lot more independent, but anything like that I would still run past them.

My dad said that I had a year to prove to him that I could make a living through Instagram and support myself financially – but he gave me the benefit of the doubt.

My mum, too, was really supportive. They both knew that I wanted different things from life, and they've always backed me 100 per cent.

I began to dedicate all my time to being an influencer: I was posting once a day, with different outfits and different backgrounds. By giving influencing a proper go, I was betting on myself – and that gamble paid off quickly. Within about a week of being home from Ibiza, I hit 20,000 followers, and from then on, that number spiralled up and up and up.

Hitting 20,000 followers on Instagram was a major milestone for me: brands started to message me to ask, 'Hey, we'd really like to work with you, what's your rate?' I didn't really know what that meant, but I spoke to a couple of other girls I knew on Instagram for advice on what I should charge. I started at about £100 for three posts, and later upped it to £200. The figure continued to rise as my follower count climbed.

PLT was one of those first companies asking me to post. They were the dream brand for any influencer to work with and always have been, so when they wanted to fit me and pay me to post (I think I started at £50 a post with them!), that was a huge moment for me. They were up-and-coming; everyone wanted to work with them or, if you weren't an influencer, wanted to work *for* them. What they represented – with the branding, the pink logo, even their fun offices in Manchester – was really current and cool. They were the 'it' brand, and they've stayed that way because the people there understand what girls like me want. So, I've worked with PLT from the very start, which is amazing, given my relationship with them now – but we'll get to that!

All this meant that, after reaching 20k followers, I was earning about £500 a month from my sponsored posts – a lot of money to me at the time. It had taken me a good while to get there, about four years, but now that I knew social media could become a job, I was going to do everything in my power to make it happen. And I've never had another job since.

So, really, it was a blessing in disguise that all that had happened with the gym – and even that Ibiza didn't work out – because it gave me the chance to do what I really wanted to do.

• • •

A few weeks after coming back from Ibiza, I had another first, as I was invited to an influencer event. I was at my dad's wedding reception, everyone dancing and drinking, when I got the DM from the hair and extension brand Beauty Works: 'We're going to a festival tomorrow and one of our girls has dropped out, we'd love you to come.' That was another 'Oh my God!' moment. There was a wedding breakfast the next day, so at first I didn't think I could make the festival. But when I told my dad about it, he encouraged me to go. He's always been so supportive of me and my career. I had no outfit ready – and that event was the sort of thing I'd normally spend months in preparation for – but I made it work. I ended up in these burgundy cargo pants with a black lacy bodysuit and black wedged boots – they were just bits and bobs that I had in my bedroom. The next day, my mum dropped me off in Essex, I had my hair and make-up done by Beauty Works, and they took us to the festival for the day, which I just loved.

> *My parents have just always*
> *been so super supportive.*

Back then, my parents would literally photograph all my Instagram content for me – my mum in particular, as I was still living with her. After a long shift at the police station, she'd come home and we'd go out together – Mum literally still in her work uniform – to shoot outfit photos somewhere like Starbucks, or at the service station in nearby Biggleswade, for my feed. Or, if we had more time, we'd go somewhere new like Cambridge for a content day, trying to get more pictures.

At first, my mum didn't really understand Instagram, but she definitely got really good at taking photos – even though it wasn't in her comfort zone to start with. We'd be shooting content – pictures and video – and my mum would get so embarrassed. People would be staring at me posing in a miniskirt and high heels in the middle of Cambridge city centre; I didn't mind it, while she'd literally want the ground to swallow her up!

But after about six months, she saw the money coming in and how happy it was making me that I was growing on Instagram, and soon it was almost second nature to her – she's really good at it! Even now, when I go home to visit, she'll still take content for me, and so will my dad and my sister. Without them, I really would not have been able to have a successful Instagram account. At the time, living where I was in Langford, I didn't really have any close friends nearby who could help me – so my family was the reason that I was able to grow and do what I did.

MAKING MY NANA PROUD

That's not to say everyone in my family has got my job from the start! It took my nana a while to really get to grips with it. We joke in my family that I've always been the grandchild that's been a bit disapproved of by the grand-parents, as I was always the one wanting to wear make-up, or have my hair done in a more grown-up way, or wear certain clothes.

For example, when I was six or seven, I always wanted my mum to crimp my hair, and whenever she did, my grandma – my dad's mum – would say, 'Why do you do that to her hair? She's too young!' While my mum's mum, my nana, would be asking me, 'Why are you wearing those nails?' Or, if I wore ripped jeans, 'What are those?!'

So, my nana never quite understood what I was up to, and it was the same with my job at first … because it does sound a bit unusual to an older person that I post photos online and get paid for it. However, once she saw me in TV adverts for PLT, she understood it a lot more … thankfully! And now she is so on board with what I do. Sadly, my dad's mum passed away, but I like to think that if she were alive today I'd be making her proud too.

These days, my job isn't as carefree, but back then, because I was doing what I loved most, it *felt* easy – even though it was still a lot of work. I was taking pictures, which I loved doing and which came easily to me, and getting paid for it. There are so many more levels to what I do now, and – wonderful though it is, don't get me wrong! – my work is much more complex and there is much more to juggle and consider. But starting out, it was just like a dream. Even my audience was at a really nice stage; as I'd find out, when you're bigger, people will actually come to your account specifically to troll, whereas back then my following was just supportive and happy to be on the journey with me. Really, it's a lesson: enjoy every stage of your journey, and don't always be trying to rush on to the next one.

MANIFESTING MANCHESTER

By that point, I was still living with my mum in Langford. It's a lovely little village, but for me, living there felt claustrophobic. I couldn't drive, so it felt like I was in the middle of nowhere. Living in Hitchin, I had been able to walk everywhere: the town centre was a 10-minute walk from home, so was the gym … everything was so close.

I started to feel isolated and suffocated. I'd now reached about 120k followers on Instagram, but I felt I couldn't really progress in my job because there weren't many new locations or cool backgrounds where I could take pictures. I wasn't networking and building relationships with businesses there, either. So, finally I decided: *I'm going to move to Manchester.*

I'd been spending quite a lot of time in the city – through the pageant world, I'd made friends with a girl who lived up there – and I'd quickly fallen in love with it. I started doing all sorts up there, staying with her or with other friends. I'd even get my lip filler there. That's really where my relationship with Manchester began, which has led to me living nearby in Cheshire now.

In the process of spending so much time there, I became even more independent. I'd take the train there all the time and stay for weeks on end before I'd come home. I was never told off for doing that; my mum would just say, 'As long as you're happy and as long as you're safe.' And I always had to have my location on my phone switched on so she could see where I was; that was the mutual agreement we had. My mum was very, very particular about always knowing where I was. She just felt better knowing that if she needed to find me, she could – that was her police officer brain coming in.

So, I thought, *I'm going to just go to Manchester*, and told my parents my plans. Within a week of me saying that, I'd found an apartment and I was gone. I just packed my stuff and left, and that was it. I always think now that Mum's never really processed that I've actually gone because it was such a quick thing! I just didn't really give her a moment to say no.

· · ·

How I got that apartment was quite a funny story: I went up to Manchester for one day to flat hunt. I did 10 viewings and hated them all; none of the properties were right. Then, as I was sat on a wall opposite a massive apartment block, eating my lunch and scrolling through Zoopla, the property website, I happened to look up for a moment.

Oh my God, I thought, *that building in front of me is incredible – I would love to live there.* It was stunning, all glass. Then I looked down to refresh the website on my phone, and a picture of that very same apartment building came up, advertising a one-bedroom apartment for £900 a month – just at random! I called the estate agent to say I was just outside, connected with them in person and walked up the stairs. I got that apartment the very same day. That was so much money and I wasn't sure that I could afford it past the first few months, but I told them I would take it. I feel like that pressure made me work harder since I knew I had to earn enough money to pay that £900 a month in rent.

I do feel like I manifested that flat, which – the way I think of it – means having enough belief in yourself that things just fall into place. Because I find that when you have enough confidence, things just happen for you; and you never doubt that they're going to happen – they *will* just happen.

I paid my first few months' rent upfront with some money I had saved up while living at home – which I was lucky to be able to do, as not everyone can do that. After that, it was going to be up to me to pay my own rent; my parents weren't going to support me. At that time I was making enough income from my Instagram to be able to live independently, but I knew it was still going to be a stretch. Again, I was striving for more than I could really achieve in that moment.

So maybe it's not a total surprise that the first night I spent in my new Manchester apartment, I felt I'd made a massive mistake. I remember it so clearly: my dad had come up with me to help me move my stuff, then he dropped me off and I was in this apartment by myself. The silence was deafening. I had that anxious feeling in my stomach, like when I was little and would go to sleepovers and would want to come home. I thought, *What have I done? Oh my God, what am I going to do? I want to go home. I hate this.*

But the next day, I went to join the gym, then I went by the city centre, and I just got out and about and slowly started to get used to it all. Eventually I fell in love with that feeling of being alone – it made me feel really independent and like the world was my oyster. I could go out anytime and do whatever I wanted, and that was a really nice feeling.

That move to Manchester was one of the best things I ever did, without a doubt. It was scary, in a way, taking the chance that I would be earning enough to pay my rent once the first few months were up. But, as I'd hoped, it was helping my career too: with so many new locations to shoot at, my following was continuing to grow.

And, though I didn't know it then, something else was about to happen that would change my life again …

STEPPING INTO THE SPOTLIGHT

INTO THE
ISLAND

Living in Manchester, I was starting to get recognised a bit, typically in a restaurant or on a night out at the sort of places my followers would go. It felt unusual for people to recognise me, but then it made me feel happy that I had that very loyal, very engaged audience. My Instagram following had grown to about 150k, and I'd been living in Manchester for about a month – not long – when I went to London to audition for a show … *Love Island*.

Even before I went for that audition, I knew I was going to be on the show that year, weird as that sounds. I had this overwhelming feeling that I'd already got the job. That wasn't a new thing either: from about 16, whenever *Love Island* was on TV, I always used to say to my family, 'I'll be on that show one day.'

'Yeah, yeah,' they'd say – but I just had this strange feeling that I was going to go on it.

At the time, it wasn't something that I was particularly aspiring to do or really desired. It was more something that, because of my influencing work, I could see myself heading towards – like I knew that was the route I'd take. Someone might say, 'No, no, you got the job because you got lucky.' But I do believe that, like my Manchester flat, I manifested it. I just believed wholeheartedly that I was going on that show.

Again, with manifesting, you have to envision yourself doing the things you want to be doing already and *then* work hard to make that vision a reality. Before I even went on the show, I saw myself being a successful businesswoman. And I just think the minute you start seeing yourself as that person and believing that you're going to get there, your focus and drive to reach that goal just become so much sharper. That attitude changes everything. For example, if you walk into an interview with the confidence and belief that you've already got the job, you're so much more likely to get it.

The minute you believe that you're already in that job you're interviewing for, or you already have that role within your workplace that you want – the moment you start believing, things happen for you.

That's not to say I didn't face any setbacks in getting there …

MY JOURNEY TO THE VILLA

The funny thing is, I had actually auditioned for *Love Island* the previous year, when I had just turned 18 and was still living with my mum. I sent off an application form and the production team asked me to come in for an audition in London. I wore red trousers and a black top – I remember it so clearly – and sat in a room with about 30 or 40 other girls, all of us waiting to be called in one by one.

In my interview, I could tell I wasn't being engaging: 'Oh, I'm Molly, I'm 18 …' I was really quiet and, looking back, just too young and not ready. I knew that I hadn't got a place on the show. I thought, *There's not a chance.* But my dad kept saying to me, 'Maybe next year, maybe you'll get it next year.'

And actually, I'm really glad I didn't get it that first time. The next year, it felt like it was the right moment. Second time around, it all unfolded so differently: I was sat at the hairdresser's – I was with my hairstylist, Emily (@emilyrosemonkhair), who I still use now and who works with Beauty Works – when I saw the DM on Instagram from one of the casting team, saying, 'We'd love you to come in for an audition.' I thought, *Oh, wow!* I don't think I was even on their radar from the previous year; it was what I'd recently been up to on social media that had brought me to their attention.

I remember saying, 'I really think this is going to be my year. I think I'm going to go on the show.' I was already believing that I was in the show and just had a really positive attitude about it.

From there it all sort of naturally fell into place. In January 2019, I went to a studio in London – they later told me I was their first audition for the series. This time around, it was a completely different audition experience. I went alone, whereas the previous year I'd taken my mum and sister. And again, I just had this overwhelming feeling of *I'm going to be on this show.*

I could tell from the way the interviewer was talking to me, and the way I was talking to her … It was just *right.* I felt like a different girl to the one who'd been in that first audition: I dressed differently, I did my make-up differently, my hair was bleach blonde (blonder than ever!) by this point – but most of all, I had so much more confidence and I knew what to say. Since my last audition, I'd moved away from home, worked on my business, lived that little bit more. I spoke about my past experiences with guys and was trying to make the crew laugh, thinking, *If I actually just woo them here, I could get this.*

In the final interview I wore a bright pink blazer with a high-necked black top and black trousers underneath, so I walked in and said, 'I've come dressed as a liquorice allsort today!' And they were laughing their heads off. I thought, *I've definitely got this!* I just had this good feeling.

Honestly, I don't know where my confidence comes from! I've always had it. Not in a cocky way, not in a big-headed way – it's never been like that. It's more, as I say, that I believe that when you want something enough, you'll get it. I went into my *Love Island* audition as someone that was already on the show, and I just had so much self-belief that I think it simply fell into place. Again, that's what I think of when I talk about manifestation: that confidence will carry you through.

And then … the show rang me and said I wasn't going to be part of their original line-up. They wanted me, but as a bombshell – which meant that I'd be joining the villa as a late arrival, to shake things up. I didn't want to do it. My friends Steph and Ellie had both been on the show themselves, and told me things to look out for, one of them being that bombshells didn't always make it onto the show as there were always quite a few of them on standby.

The TV team was trying to persuade me otherwise, telling me I'd be the first bombshell to go in, and I thought, *Nah.* I was pretty sceptical about it. Things were going well for me business-wise: my Instagram was growing rapidly and organically. I knew that I could go on the show and potentially damage that – if you say something wrong, you could ruin your reputation. So, it was a lot to think about. A lot of people were saying to me, 'You don't really need it. You can do this without it.'

I listened to all that … and decided that I'd do it anyway!

WHY I REALLY WENT IN

I didn't think I would find love on the show. Don't get me wrong, I was obviously hopeful that I would, but I did not go on there relying on definitely finding a man. I was also open to the exciting opportunity of spending my summer away – and I've been quite open about this on my YouTube. I knew that being on a TV show like *Love Island* could raise my profile, and I was focusing on building my audience, so eventually I decided that going on there felt like a risk worth taking. After all, there are definitely easier ways to find a boyfriend! But I could see the potential that going on the show held for me, in terms of giving me another platform.

After all, I'd already seen how my Instagram had benefitted from me having a presence on YouTube. As I mentioned, my Instagram audience was really engaged. What that means is this: when you have a following on Instagram, the typical percentage of your audience that should be engaging with your posts – liking them, for example – is around 10 per cent. So, when I had 150,000 followers, I should have been getting around 15,000 likes on each post. Instead, I was averaging 30,000, which means I had 20 per cent engagement – huge! At the time, I had around 30,000 subscribers to my YouTube channel, and I knew that was driving my higher engagement – because people knew the person behind the Instagram pictures.

So, if YouTube could do that ... what would a TV show do?

I decided to take it. Annoyingly, I had to decide before I went on the show if I wanted to take out another six months on my Manchester flat, and I had decided to do that, hoping that I'd make enough money when I came out to pay for it. Then on May 25, the day before my birthday, I flew out to Majorca, where the show was filmed. Spending my birthday abroad seemed to have become a bit of a pattern for me!

I turned 20 in a remote town up a mountain, surrounded by goats, hidden away from the press ahead of going into the villa you see on TV.

I couldn't call my mum or my sister and, to be honest, I was all over the place. I spent two weeks there in total, then I went on the show as the first bombshell ... and it all happened from there. Which all goes to prove how what starts as a 'no' can lead somewhere very different in the end.

I'll always remember walking into the villa in a little black dress, in a clip that went a bit viral and still circulates now. That was a really powerful moment for me – one of the best moments of my life, in fact; I love watching it back – because I felt like I was just so ready for it. And I was excited! I knew my life was never going to be the same after I walked into that villa.

This was the start of a brand-new chapter – I just didn't know what it was going to bring.

MY HIGHLIGHT REEL

Obviously, the main highlight and the reason for all my incredible memories of that TV experience was that I did find my boyfriend in there. Tommy and I felt almost meant to be in so many ways: I found out that he lived five minutes away from me in Manchester, we're both born in May, and we're the exact same age. I also met Maura in there, who's one of my best friends now.

I love that I have the moment I met my forever partner on video to share with my kids one day.

'How did you and Dad meet?'

'Oh, I'll show you …!'

That's really nice. I'm so blessed and lucky to have been able to have that experience. But in terms of the very first meeting – when Tommy and I shared a hot tub on our first 'date' – I've not watched that specific part back that many times, because I find it quite cringey: our conversation was actually mortifying! But it's really nice to watch back other clips, from challenges to our first kiss. What I see on-screen does match up with my memories – how it felt to be in those moments – pretty well.

I had decided, before I went into the villa, that I wasn't going to do anything on camera that I wouldn't do in public. But obviously, while we were in there, Tommy and I were getting really, really close. I hadn't expected it, but I now had a boyfriend! And when I came out, the fact that my love life had been on national telly was never a problem with my family – I never really spoke about it with them (thank goodness) or anyone else in my life, so it wasn't an issue. But I can't watch those scenes back!

WHAT YOU DIDN'T SEE

That all being said … *Love Island* was challenging at times over those eight weeks in the villa. Maybe because I met Tommy and Maura, people don't realise that. Don't get me wrong, it was a great experience – but it was more difficult in there than people may think.

For someone like me, who was already my own boss and used to running my own life, it was a shock to find, suddenly, you don't know when you're going to bed, you don't know when you're waking up, you don't really even have control over your meals. I actually never knew the hour of the day the whole time I was there. There are no clocks in the villa – even the one on the oven was covered up – so you lose all concept of time. Each morning, we would wake up, brush our teeth and then go down and sit on the beanbags in the garden, waiting to have a conversation they'd want to air, or to do one of the show's challenges. I don't mean any of this in a bad way – they were making a TV show, and that is a time-consuming, complicated process – but it was a challenging two months for me.

I'd also been away from home an extra two weeks before all that – the longest I'd ever been away from my family and friends. Bearing in mind, too, that my phone was my job, so it was never out of my sight, and then I had it taken away from me for 11 weeks altogether. I didn't enjoy having time off from it! We were given special phones to use while we were in there: we couldn't use them like normal phones, but I was taking pictures every day of me and Tommy, the girls, me in the mirror. The show sent a few from the camera roll to my sister, who posted them on my Instagram.

I definitely learned a lot; being there changed me as a person. I learned how to be away from home for that length of time and to deal with feeling homesick. I wasn't about to leave, so I just had to bear that feeling and be OK with it.

And I had to learn to be fine without my phone, if needs be. (Although, I don't think I'd go another few months without it!

My mum and dad will still say to me, 'Get off your phone,' and to some people it might look like I'm being antisocial, but the reality is, I run a business from it.)

Obviously, because I met Tommy, it made it all a lot easier. But I can imagine for the girls that don't find someone who they get really close to in there, it can be really hard.

FIRST TASTE OF TROLLING

If I thought being inside the villa was tough, I was about to find out that life outside of it could be challenging in a very different way.

My sister, Zoe, had been managing my socials while I was in the villa. Because she knew me so well, she knew what I'd want to be put on Instagram, so she was in charge. But the hate got so bad when I was in there – the trolling really was on another level – that a friend of mine recommended Fran, who's now my manager. She and her team really helped Zoe. They worked closely together, and my family fell in love with Fran.

Of course, I didn't know any of this. Meanwhile, new bomb-shells were coming into the villa saying, 'Oh, you're managed by Fran, of The Social PR?' (They'd seen Fran's email in my bio on my socials.) I didn't know who that was, so I was freaking out to the producers, saying, 'You need to tell me now what's going on with my Instagram because this is my job. My family are meddling with my job!'

It wouldn't have mattered so much if I weren't such a perfectionist with my Instagram, but I thought that my family had appointed a new manager without asking me for no good reason, and I didn't know what was going on – it was awful. But the producers wouldn't tell me anything.

Then, as part of the show, the Islanders get to see their relatives, and my mum and sister came onto the show to visit me. I tried to find out what was happening. 'What's going on with my Instagram? Who's this person who's managing me?' But they just said they'd tell me when I came out and I was so frustrated.

My sister, bless her, knew how much I wanted to know what was happening with my business. I was looking at her, saying, 'Zoe, what's going on – how many followers have I got?'

Quietly, she drew the shape of 2.2 – for 2.2 million – on her leg. I was stunned. Oh my God! I remember her nodding: It's good. *But I did also get a sense of* It's good and it's bad; it's a lot.

What that meant, I found out on the day of the final. Before the live final ceremony itself, Tommy and I were watching TV – we weren't meant to, but the crew had forgotten to take the remote out of our bedroom! So we watched a breakfast TV show, where they were talking about *Love Island*, of all things.

At that point, I think it's fair to say that the general feeling inside the villa was that Tommy and I had probably won. Because we were the only people in the show that had connected the way we had, become girlfriend and boyfriend, and had this story in the way we had, it maybe seemed the most likely outcome. (Of course, we'd end up as the runners-up to Amber and Greg. I honestly didn't care – I was happy for them – because for me, it had never been about winning. I already felt like I'd won because I had met Tommy, and I'd never expected to get a boyfriend and to leave the show together.)

Then I watched that breakfast TV segment … and that changed everything. The message was: everyone hates Molly, she cries crocodile tears, she's fake, she doesn't like Tommy, she's only in there for the money. It was really, really, really savage. Tommy and I just sat there watching TV, feeling like … *Oh.*

After all that time, suddenly I wasn't ready to get my phone back and connect with the outside world. I was scared. I thought, *All of that's been going on – what have I done wrong?* Because I didn't think I'd done anything wrong, but clearly people hadn't engaged with me the way I'd hoped or the way I'd thought they had. Today, I feel quite differently about all that – as I'll explain later. But back in that hotel room, in the moment where I saw that segment, I really was thinking, *Oh gosh, what's happening?*

There were a few other moments that underlined just what was ahead. Just before the final, we all left the villa to go and get ready in a hotel. There was a lot of security around, but at one point Tommy and I were in a lift together. The doors opened and there were two young boys stood outside. Their faces literally dropped

Me with Grandma and Pop Pops.

Above is me, Zoe and Dad. I loved going through these images for the book. So many precious memories!

Above is Mum, Zoe and me. My mum is the keeper of the family photos. She also coordinated our purple outfits this day.

My mom always used to make us homemade birthday cakes.

Everyone in the family
knows how important
Ellie Belly is to me!

Me and the family on our annual trip to France
to remember my grandad's time in the war.

I loved our family vacations. This is another one of us having fun in France.

Zoe and me on a trip to London.

Classic school pictures.
I always had a full fringe to
hide my birthmark when I
was at school.

to the floor, like they couldn't believe what they were seeing. I think for them, it was probably more about Tommy than me! But that really resonated with me: *Oh my God, people know who my boyfriend is. They're going to know who I am. This is actually what things are going to be like now.*

By this point, I was really nervous and fearful about what I was about to face when I would finally be given my phone back. Mine wasn't even really working at the start – it was basically broken by having to start up again after being turned off for so long! In the meantime, my Instagram had gone from 160k to nearly 3 million followers. How does your phone even begin to catch up with that?

It was the best feeling in the world to get it back – but also a bit of a reality check, even then. Because as much as I was so happy to have my phone back, as Tommy and I were sitting on our beds on our phones, I realised, *Real life's back.* Before, we'd have been talking to each other, because we had nothing else to do. That bubble bursts so quickly: real life hits the moment you get your phone back, and that's it – you're out of your little dreamland that never really existed.

After all, in what world would you spend eight weeks with the guy you just met, sharing a bed straight away, no phones, no family, no one there? It just doesn't happen. I'd not even Instagram-stalked Tommy before I met him! It was like a blind date.

Now, it was time to get back to the real world.

BACK TO
REALITY

As soon as I got my phone back, I spoke to my family and all my friends – I wanted to call everyone at the same time – and finally talking to them again was amazing.

Looking at Twitter was not so fun. For days, #Money-Mae was trending because people thought I was just there for the £50,000 prize money. Now, it's all a bit of a joke: my nickname with my friends and family is 'Money-Mae'. But back then, it was a whole new world to me; seeing myself trending on Twitter was a hard thing to wrap my head around. I couldn't believe people even knew my name, let alone that they were writing about me.

Still, that was more shocking to me than offensive – there were worse things they could have said! Obviously, people commenting about my looks was quite hard to swallow, because I had never had to deal with anybody really attacking me over that before. But the only really hard thing to read was some of the stuff about me and Tommy: I didn't like that some people were saying they thought our relationship was fake, because I knew that it was very real.

And from the get-go, I've always dealt with all that quite well, I'd say. At the time, the press was actually saying that I had security because of how bad the hate was online. I didn't at all – I was with my family and with Tommy and I was totally fine. And while some of it was hard to see when I first came out of the villa, because everything else was so amazing – I was seeing my family and so many great things were happening – I felt it all balanced out.

Anyway, I had other things to be thinking about. That time of my life, straight out of the show, is such a blur that I can barely remember what happened day-to-day. I'd do anything to get to relive those weeks because they were just so insane. My whole life had changed overnight, and suddenly so many people knew who I was – you can't prepare someone for that. It was just wild.

And I had a lot to do. When I flew back to England, Fran came with my family to the airport. I was really sceptical and a bit annoyed with my family that they'd done this: 'You can't decide who my manager is – it just doesn't work like that!' Then I met Fran and I just fell in love with her instantly, like they had. We all went to a hotel in Milton Keynes – why Milton Keynes? I don't know! – and she had actually created this folder for me to look at over the next week of all the different brand deals that had come in and how my year could look if I took certain deals, how it might look if I took others. It just felt right, so I told her, 'Yeah, you've got the job!'

And that was it. I don't think anyone really realises how huge a part of my life Fran is now. Everything I do happens because of me, but she helps me make things happen. Fran's like the business part of my brain – she's very smart with that kind of thing.

Soon after getting back, I ended up staying in a hotel in London, the May Fair, for about three weeks, where I was really busy with business meetings with fashion brands. Meanwhile, Fran took control of dealing with the media. She has incredible relationships with a lot of journalists, so I didn't really have to worry about that side of things much because I had her. Everything I'd ever dreamt of was just coming true.

When I wasn't working, Tommy met my family properly, including coming to my mum's house for a curry. Mum loved him from the get-go – she always jokes that she fancies him: 'Tommy, you know you should be with me instead of Molly, stop pretending.' That's just my mum's sense of humour! But both my parents adore Tommy. He's the dream guy to take home, so I knew that they were going to love him. And with his career as a boxer, no one's ever going to trouble me if he's next to me. He's a very protective person and very loyal and kind, and he butters my mum up the right way.

Of course, I met Tommy's parents, too. They live in Salford, so I met them when we moved up to my flat in Manchester. Now, I see them basically every other day, whereas when Tommy sees my parents it's more of a special occasion because I don't get the chance to go home that often because of my busy schedule.

A DIFFERENT LIFE

One of the first things Tommy and I did as a couple, in those first few weeks in London, was to go out to TGI Friday's and the cinema, because we both love that – and we were really certain about wanting a date night. I just wanted to do something normal with him, and he felt the same. It's nice that we did that because I look back now, and I'll always remember doing it. We planned to go to the TGI's in Leicester Square then to the Vue cinema just across the way to see a film.

At the restaurant, we got absolutely hounded – it was not a smart thing to do because it was huge and busy, one of the most central TGI restaurants in London. Everyone was looking over at us, coming over to our table, trying to get pictures. We weren't really bothered because it was a new world – 'Of course you can have a picture' – and it was just a privilege that anyone was asking us. But we were both thinking, *What on earth?* That level of attention's never really changed for us, especially because Tommy is tall; whenever we go out anywhere, people notice him straight away! Plus, we have two very different audiences, which means we're on the radar of a lot of people when we're out together. Both Tommy's boxing fans and my Instagram fans will come over, which means double the people, in a way.

The cinema was fine because nobody really noticed us in the dark. But during the film, I had a massive nosebleed. That was something that kept happening during those first few weeks – the first time I was having my hair done after leaving the show, I had another nosebleed. I don't normally suffer from them, so that was weird. After that dinner and cinema date, Fran said to me, 'Molly, you can't just be doing things like that. You can't just be going off to TGI Friday's anymore. We'd need to get you security.' I was beginning to realise that things really weren't just the same. I couldn't just go about and expect to fly under the radar and never have to deal with paparazzi, so I just had to try to find my feet a bit with it.

Looking back, the nosebleeds were a sign of the underlying anxiety I was feeling because so much was going on, and my head was so scrambled – they were most definitely from me just trying to take everything in, and the stress I felt around everything that was happening. I was learning that even things you want to happen – that you're excited about – can feel stressful when they do. As I've always felt, the good can come with a bit of bad, and vice versa.

As for Tommy through all this? He was just cool as a cucumber; nothing could really bother him! I could lean on him if I was finding anything hard – with the media or whatever. He's got a very different approach to it to me, in that he doesn't care at all what people say about him. He's just not bothered. So, when I find things hard, he's really good at calming me down. He always levels me out and makes me realise, actually, I don't need to be worried about that stuff. Sometimes he's almost a bit too cool about it and then sometimes I'm a bit too dramatic – so together we find that nice happy medium, where we level each other out.

About a week after coming out of the show, I hit 3 million followers on Instagram, while I reached 500,000 subscribers on YouTube. That was a really clear reminder to me that I just wanted to do what I was doing before, but now with these new followers. And that's exactly what I went back to, almost straight away. I'd had a bit of a break when I first came out – in fact, everyone thought Tommy and I had broken up. Then I posted a picture of him and me at the May Fair, before the finale of *Love Island*'s sister show, *Aftersun*.

Things had been crazy busy, which explained why I hadn't posted until then – but it was also strategic in a way, because the silence got everyone talking: 'What's going on?!' When we posted this picture, it felt like *boom!* It did exactly what I wanted it to do. Everyone was talking about it and sharing it. It went viral, with 1.3 million likes as of now, which is insane. It's still probably the most-liked picture on my Instagram feed.

But more importantly, getting back to what I loved doing helped me through that crazy time, and soon I was feeling a lot more myself. From then on, I started posting every day again, and basically have done ever since.

HOW I FEEL ABOUT
THE SHOW NOW

Without a doubt, *Love Island* is how a lot of people got to know me. My time in the villa was an eight-week period of my life where I met my boyfriend and had a really exciting summer. But I don't feel like that defines me. Everyone from the show deals with things differently and goes on to take different paths. It's all a learning experience.

Personally, I've not really spoken much about my experience since then, because I've tended to focus more on what I'm doing in the present. I've always wanted to be known for the things that I've done with fashion brands and hair companies and my own tanning company.

People misinterpret what I've done as 'She thinks she's better than everyone.' That's very much a misconception. Don't get me wrong: I wouldn't be here today – or, at least, I wouldn't be exactly where I am – without *Love Island*. I totally acknowledge that.

But since the show, I've made choices and taken risks that have made my platform what it is today. It's uniquely mine, and I'm so proud of that.

Even before the show, I was giving my all to make my dreams come true. I was trying to build my following. I was positioning myself and planning for the future. Who's to say what that would have come to? I guess I'll never know!

LOVE AND FRIENDSHIP

FRIENDSHIP
LESSONS

These days, I can count the people in my innermost circle on one hand – but I've never been the sort of girl that is in loads of massive friendship groups.

Growing up, I'd go to the cinema with friends and things like that, but I was so busy with all my activities, I never really had a lot of time to socialise. Like a lot of kids, I didn't love sleepovers anyway – like I've said, I'd get there and get that sick, anxious feeling and just want to come home! The parents would always have to call my mum back to pick me up.

It actually took a while for my anxiety around sleeping somewhere unfamiliar to go away fully – not until my parents' divorce, in fact, when I had to quickly get OK with going to stay in my dad's new flat. So, I've always been that person that hasn't had loads of girlfriends around me; as long as my family was proud of me, that's all that really mattered to me. I can definitely survive without having a large group of friends.

I also feel I don't do well with a big circle because I can't really give everyone my time, and I want to be a better friend than that. Plus, I don't like drama – it's really something that I just always like to stay out of – and I feel like when you have a large friendship group, drama often comes with that. So, I keep my very closest circle to about five people, being my family, Fran and Tommy – that's pretty much it! Those are the people I'd call if I had a problem. Obviously, it's nice to speak to your boyfriend about things, but sometimes you want to have a girl's opinion, so I'll call Zoe or Fran for that. Fran's not only my manager but my friend; it's good to be able to relate on that level, where you know she would feel the same way if something happened to her.

As for me and my sister, Zoe and I are really close. I can honestly say anything I want to her and she wouldn't even bat an eyelid. Zoe's the person who knows my deepest secrets, and I know she wouldn't say a thing – I can trust her with anything and everything. Even now, every single Instagram picture I take, I send it to Zoe before I post it and I always ask if she likes it, because she's so honest with me. She's not afraid to say, 'No, I hate it, take it again.' She's just that person that I'll always be able to lean on and know that she has my back. At the PLT party to celebrate me becoming their creative director (more on that later!), they played a video of my journey with the brand, and Zoe was literally bawling her eyes out, crying with pride, because she's seen my dreams come to life.

Still, we may sound sweet and lovely now, but, wow, when I say we used to argue and fight, we had some real tiffs growing up! Because we were so different, like chalk and cheese – still are, with her in the army and me doing what I do – we could clash. But now, she's really happy to take me for who I am: she understands that we're very different and that she's never going to be able to change me – and vice versa. I'm just so lucky to have her.

MY INNER CIRCLE

As well as that close circle, I'm really lucky to have a very small group of friends that back me 110 per cent – they're the kind of friends that I'm so glad I have around me.

From home in Hertfordshire, I have Grace and Natalie, who are really lovely girls who are not bothered about Instagram and things like that. Grace works for her family's kitchen business and Natalie's family run a local chip shop. They're just two friends I'll always be able to trust and love. They didn't go to the same school as me, but we're from the same area, so it's really nice I've still got them. They're really the only two people that I have kept in touch with from my 'old' life.

Then, some of my best friends now I've met through Instagram: other influencers. In the early days, I made a lot of friends online. We'd be commenting on each other's feeds, DMing each other, just girls supporting girls and building each other up, then we'd go to influencer events and meet each other in person there. We all supported one another – which, really, is the secret of networking.

Whatever you're doing, whether that's starting a business or working on an Instagram page, the people you'll come into contact with through that will tend to be quite like-minded, because you share the same interests. The relationships you have with them just gradually build, and then you meet each other at an event, and before you know it you've networked without even realising it. 'Networking' is a scary word to a lot of people, but it doesn't have to be!

One of those girls I've already mentioned briefly: Stephanie Lam, who was on *Love Island* before me. Steph actually lived in St Albans, which is near where I grew up in Hitchin, but I got to know her when I was up in Manchester at events. We realised pretty quickly that we were from a similar area and just had loads in common. So when we went back home, we'd occasionally take content together, and then we both moved to Manchester permanently at a similar time. We became really tight, and to this day she's one of my closest friends. I'm really lucky that she lives just down the road from me now and that we get to see each other all the time.

Then, of course, from my own stint on the show, I have Maura. Of course, on *Love Island* she was interested in Tommy for a bit, but there's just no issue there. After Tommy started getting closer with me, she said to me: 'Look, I'll never go near him again in that way, you know,' and ever since then we've been best friends. She comes up here all the time to stay with me, and I go down and stay with her in Essex. She and Tommy are really good friends as well. They're like brother and sister – they make fun of each other 24/7. I get a lot of questions when I do Q and As along the lines of: 'How are you comfortable with Maura being friends with Tommy? Isn't it weird to you?' But when you have a friend like Maura you have that complete trust.

As for why we click, we are really different – again, like Zoe and me, we always say we're chalk and cheese – but we just get along so well. She loves to go out and have fun, but she's also happy to chill with me a lot, and I will go out with her for dinner or whatever. Likewise, she's a few years older, but she acts (and looks!) super young, while a lot of people say that I act a bit old for my age. So it just works between us. We have gone our own ways work-wise, as well: she chooses a lot more TV work while I've gone down more of the fashion route. We deal with a lot of the same things in terms of the press, and we both take our work seriously, but we definitely have our own lanes, and we just support each other massively.

And I'm good friends with the girls who work with Fran, too – Erin and Ellen.

So, I definitely don't have a girl group. Instead, I have friends from all different backgrounds – which is totally fine, whatever you might think your friendships *should* look like.

Honestly, the one time I struggle with it is on birthdays. I worry about this person and I worry about that person, because they're all from different parts of my life, so I'm not sure if they're going to gel with each other when they come together for me. But really, it's kind of nice, because I feel like I've got people from every part of my life: girls from my old life, girls from my new life – and they're all good.

Still, that's not to say that I've kept every friendship – that's just not realistic.

WHY I DON'T GET FOMO

I'm not a social butterfly. It's weird for me to say that, because people might think I am because of my job, but I'm not really into going for dinners and drinks and socialising – it's just not for me.

I think a lot of people need to have that time out of their working life to go and have a glass of wine with their friends. I have friends who work all week and then, at the weekend, all they want to do is go out and socialise. That's not how I like to spend my weekends. Now, I totally see why someone else might love and need that. The thing is, when I don't have to make chat, I won't. I think because my job is so eyes-on-you – and part of that is to be smiley and bubbly when I'm out at events – when I can just be quiet and chilled, I always take that opportunity with both hands.

So, I very rarely feel FOMO. If I see that someone's on holiday or doing something equally relaxing, then I might feel a twinge … But I don't really feel like I want to be somewhere with people when I see they're all socialising, especially now that my job involves being at events. The times I feel the most relaxed and happiest are not when I'm out socialising; they're when I'm at home, doing absolutely nothing. I don't know if that will change for me. But right now, going out is just not a priority. Because I am so career-minded, my social life has taken a little bit of a backseat in a way, but then again I have friends who like to work hard and play hard too. Ultimately, it's just about working out what suits you personally.

My focus is just on work and my relationship
and my family – those are my top priorities.

And I'm OK with that. I get more of a kick out of an incredible work trip than a big night out! Making polite conversation with people I don't know well just doesn't relax me – so, when I don't have to, small talk is not what I want to do.

Still, by now, I genuinely could make conversation with a brick wall if I needed to! The trick is, it's easier to turn it around on the other person and ask them questions. I already talk about my life all day, every day, on social media, so I can't be talking about it anymore! So, my advice for socialising with people you don't know is to take control of the conversation and ask questions, and let the other person do their thing.

Don't get me wrong, I do like to have friends around me, but I just like things to be casual and not forced at all. I don't feel relaxed and content when I'm out making small talk; I feel relaxed and content when I'm at home, surrounded by people that I know. I love having people around me where it just feels effortless – and I can be totally myself.

THE PRESSURE TO FIT IN

Even though I know what I want from my friendships and social life now, it has taken me a while to work it all out. When you're at school, it can feel like being cool is everything – you'll do anything just to fit in with the popular group and sit at the popular table in the corner. That's all I wanted to do when I was younger – I wanted to be popular!

At secondary school, I was in a group of girls that weren't the quietest, but we weren't necessarily the really cool group, either. And I really do remember just desperately wanting to be like one of the popular girls. I used to think, *God, I'd do anything to be* that *girl instead of me*, as being part of the cool group felt so important back then. I always reflect on that now – how, if I'd actually got my wish and swapped lives with one of them, I wouldn't have been happy. Instead, I have ended up just where I needed to be. Of course, when you're younger, you're not so rational, and you want what you don't have.

The funny thing is, it took me a few years, but I ended up on that popular table in the end, for years 10 and 11 (years 7, 8 and 9, I didn't make the cut …!). By that stage, I'd got rid of my braces, I didn't have short hair anymore, and I'd dyed my hair blonde. So, maybe I'd started to look the part of that 'cool girl', even if that wasn't really me, deep down. Now, I'm not really in touch with anybody from school. Even then, I was very aware that your school friends are your school friends and when you move on – as I did, to fashion school – relationships will often change.

While being in a certain crowd can feel so important at the time, gradually you learn what you really want from your relationships and the people around you. You realise that you don't have to force yourself to like things that other people like if they're just not *you*.

And whenever I have tried to force myself, it's been a complete mistake.

For example, I only went to work that season in Ibiza because my friends were doing it. I thought, *Well, if my friends are doing a season in Ibiza, I should go and like it – I need to go and drink and fit in.* Everyone I mentioned it to reacted the same way, telling me I was the last person in the world who should go off and do that: 'You'll absolutely hate it! You hate alcohol. You hate partying. You hate late nights. Why are you going to Ibiza?'

I thought, *Because everyone's always telling me not to do it, I'm going to go and do it and I'm going to love it. I'm going to prove them wrong. And I'm going to come back every single summer for the next 10 years!*

I really wanted to make it work. So I went and, as I said, everyone was right: it was not my scene at all. I think people out there thought of me as 'the stuck-up girl' because I wasn't getting involved. Of course, I was never going to touch drugs, but I had hoped doing the season would force me to like alcohol and having fun with friends in that way. It didn't – I just wanted to be in bed, watching films. I've always been that way. Even my mum was saying, 'Don't come home yet – you've got to give it a proper chance.' But I thought, *I can't be around this, I feel like I'm letting my parents down,* so I thought it was the right thing to do to go home.

When I told my manager at the beach club, they were quite nasty to me about it: 'There's so many girls that would die for this opportunity.' But it just wasn't me and I wasn't changing my mind. I didn't even tell anyone else I was leaving; after my shift I just packed my stuff, got on the plane and went. I had lasted two weeks, and I was so happy to be home – I'd hated every minute of it. Not for me!

In a similar way, when I moved to Manchester, I made myself go out on the weekends to make friends. I'd go to Chinawhite, the cool club to go to on a Saturday night, with a couple of Instagram influencer girlfriends and have a few drinks with them.

Looking back at the handful of times I got drunk during that period, I don't think, *That night was really great.* Loads of my friends always have the best time going out, but personally, I would wake up the next day with a terrible hangover and a lot of regret, feeling awful and embarrassed about things I'd said or things that I wouldn't have done if I'd been in my right mind. Especially now, being in the public eye, it's just scary to me – the thought of doing something stupid on a night out. You know when your friends say, 'I'm dying to go out and have a drink'? I've never, ever felt the need to do that. So, by now, I've accepted that drinking and clubbing just aren't my thing. The most I would ever do is have a pink gin and lemonade or a pornstar martini, but those are when I am celebrating something, not all the time. I have no judgement for the people who do love partying, but I found that it just wasn't for me, and that's OK.

*If you like watching Harry Potter on a
weekend and eating a Nando's with your
favourite person and not leaving the sofa,
that's OK to do on your Saturday!
You don't have to go to a club.*

The only major arguments Tommy and I have had have been to do with him drinking, which he only does a few times a year. He won't even do anything wrong; I'll just lose it at him because I hate it. I do have this anxiety around alcohol and the things I've seen it do to the people around me – I personally don't think that alcohol adds anything good to a situation. In my experience, yes, it might temporarily make you have a better night out, but the next day you're suffering the repercussions when you have a terrible hangover.

Maybe I've just never had a good experience with it. But over time, I've realised a lot of things about myself. It's OK to prioritise what you like to do – and of course it's totally fine if that involves having a big night out! Do whatever *you* enjoy and makes you happy. It's just that I've realised that for me, drinking and partying isn't really it.

TRUST ISSUES

I do feel like a lot of my followers, as well as the people that are in my life, know the real me. What I wouldn't share with my audience is minimal. In fact, it's something that I've always struggled with a little bit: holding things back that I should hold back. And sometimes I've said things to people around me that I'm not necessarily close with, then thought, *Oh, God, I shouldn't have said that!* That's something that's happened on an almost daily basis at times. I'm not someone that's naturally good at hiding things or being a closed-off person, but it is something I have become more conscious of over time: that sometimes you have to be careful what you say.

> *Sometimes I have said things that I shouldn't say, I have given away things that I shouldn't have given away, and I have trusted people I shouldn't trust.*

It's been hard; my followers really bond with me *because* I talk about the arguments I have with Tommy, or because I talk about the fact that I'm about to wear a bikini and I've not shaved my bikini line. I talk about everything, and that makes me relatable to other girls – they want a girl who's willing to share the things that aren't perfect.

I don't instinctively hide anything; if I don't get a job, I'll say on YouTube, 'I had a really bad day today, I was up for an amazing job and I didn't get it, so I'm really upset' – whereas a lot of influencers would choose to not share that. And I probably wouldn't change that side of me because it's helped me build a relationship with my followers. I'm not just that one-dimensional girl on Instagram. When you go onto my YouTube, I don't hold back! In the same way, opening up and sharing all sides of yourself might help you build deeper relationships in your own life.

Still, being too open has affected me sometimes. Say, I've been with friends I'm not close to and I've talked about private things I've got coming up with work … and then I have that moment of thinking, *You know* that *person, who knows* that *person, who works for* that *business … Hang on a minute, I should not have said that!* So it can come around to bite you in the bum.

Someone could tell me something, and I would never ever use that to stab them in the back – but sometimes I forget that not everybody has the same mindset. The way I deal with things is not the way someone else might deal with them. I've had to learn that I can confide in the people in my circle – but I can't trust everybody.

HOW I (DON'T!) HANDLE CONFLICT

Anyone who's close to me knows that I don't do well with conflict. Even with stupid, small things where, say, I need to speak to someone about something for work, I can struggle. Back in the early days, when Fran and I were first building our relationship, if I ever actually needed to say, 'I want it done this way', I wouldn't be able to tell her because I was so petrified!

I do really struggle not just with confrontation but even just the awkwardness of having to say how I really feel – having to say, 'Actually, I'm not happy with this. I'd like it to be this way.'

When I first started shooting with PLT, I was a bit more shy about giving my feedback and it used to be a running joke that even if I wasn't totally happy with what was happening on the day, I wouldn't tell anyone. Their creative manager would always ask me, 'Are you happy with everything going on?'

'Yeah, yeah, yeah …' I would reply.

'Well, even if you aren't,' she'd say, 'I know you wouldn't tell me, so I'm just going to hope that you are!' Because everyone knew that I'm a bit of a people-pleaser. But the more I have grown as a person and into my role as creative director at PLT, I have definitely learned how to speak my mind and share my thoughts with the team, and I actually love being able to give my input to make the shoots as amazing as they can be.

Whenever I do have any conflict with someone, I get the same feeling I would when my parents would have arguments when I was younger: that sort of sick, stomach-in-knots feeling that I've mentioned before – almost anxiety over the idea of conflict. So maybe that's got something to do with it … or maybe I just don't like arguments! The only people I can properly argue with are Tommy and Zoe. (Maybe it's because I'm so close to them both – I know that it's not going to be a massive deal. Or maybe, when it comes to Tommy and me, my mum's got it right: she thinks it's all about the passion in our relationship, because one thing we do is make up really quickly!)

I'm still not good with conflict, but over time I have developed my own ways of dealing with it. If I feel like I'm going to have an altercation with someone, or even if I just want to say something that might not go down too well, I'll plan out in my head what I want to say before I come out with it. I'll sit on it for a while and think, *Do I definitely want to say this, do I definitely want to say it like this?* So, for example, I won't just say off the cuff, 'I don't want to do this.' In the moment, I'll think, *Oh, I actually don't want to do this …* And then I'll consider afterwards, *How can I word this? Should I text it?*

That's the other thing I do – if I decide I *do* want to say something, I might send a text or a voice note (that I can delete and do over if I want to). Because sometimes my voice goes really nervous when I'm addressing something face-to-face with someone: I'll try to speak and nothing will come out, or it does … but really shaky-sounding! I remember once, I wanted to tell Fran about something – I can't even remember what it was – and I was on the phone to her. Of course, I've known for her years, but my voice was literally trembling – it was weird. I thought, *I will never do that ever again – I'm just going to text what I want to say or record a voice note that at least I can redo if I need to!*

Similarly, I'm not someone who tends to just explode, either. If I'm having a bad day, I will let out what I'm feeling but only if I'm with people that I can trust and I feel comfortable with – Tommy or my sister or my mum. Then I would! But I never really row with friends. What I *do* do is write texts that I never send, because I can't deal with the fallout! I write down what I want to say … and then I just delete it. I'd rather write it in my Notes app than have the aggro of starting a bit of an argument when it wasn't a big issue. I've even done that instead of tweeting something, and then at least I've got it out of my system without any unwanted consequences.

WHEN FRIENDSHIPS END

In recent years, I've definitely faced a few incidents of people wanting to be friends with me for what they can gain. And I've definitely lost some friendships after seeing a different side to people. I don't think some people ever expected me to go off and do what I have. A lot of people viewed me as this girl that would always be a smaller influencer, then the next thing they knew, I went on TV and came out with a much bigger following, which then kept growing. I think some of the people in my life didn't know how to handle that – at first, I didn't really know how to handle the change, either.

When you come out of a show like that, it sounds cliché, but you really do see who your friends are. I remember, for the first collection I did with PLT, we threw a huge party where I realised that not all of my friends were happy for me and my newfound success. Of course, I had plenty of friends who were unconditionally supportive, but there were some who seemed to be bothered that I had been catapulted into a new world. I didn't want to believe it, but maybe they weren't the friends I thought they were. It upset me, but it was also a good reminder that, really, how people react to your success is all about them, not you.

And the friends that I had who were so chilled about it all; who knew that they weren't going to get a reply from me for weeks; who, if they were my home friends, I now lived four hours away from; and who didn't distance themselves from me because of all that … they added up to a very small number of people. I never had a big circle, so it wasn't as if I actively eliminated people! But with some of those who I was more acquaintances with, we did sort of naturally part ways – while my true friends just carried on the journey with me. They were all so supportive, so I was really lucky.

> ## Real friends don't change when you find success – they're just supportive.

Of course, it's not always low key when a friendship ends. I actually fell out with a very good friend of mine recently, someone I'd describe as a best friend. We had been really, really close but completely grew apart, and now we're not friends anymore. It was all a bit tricky: she felt I was unsupportive because I'm not always great at keeping in contact with people … but we had both changed. Every day I was waking up thinking, *Is this the day that our friendship's gonna end? Is this the day that we're going to have the big fallout?* That's not how you're meant to be with your friends. Friends are supposed to add to your life, so that you really *want* to see them, you *want* to hang out with them – and that's partly why my circle is so small, because I don't feel that with everyone.

I'm still grieving that friendship and think about her most days, so falling out with her was really a significant event in my life. It has really underlined for me that people and relationships can change, no matter how close you may be in the first place. I do like to think that everything happens for a reason, and I am not rigid about closing chapters in my life – I don't hold grudges – so who knows?

> *I still get upset about that friendship ending now. The end of a friendship can be like a breakup: you have to really process that you've lost someone in your life, you're not going to speak to them anymore, and you're not going to know what they're up to.*

But sometimes a friendship ending can be for the best – if you're really not getting on with someone, if they're not adding positivity to your life and making you happy, then they need to go (and if it's got to that stage, it's probably not working for them either!). If anything in life doesn't work for you, it needs to go, if possible – I am such a strong believer in that you get just one life, so every day needs to be the best it can be. And that doesn't mean that everyone's 'best version' has to be the same. Make it what you want it to be.

The reality is that you don't hold on to every friendship – and that's not necessarily a bad thing; that's just life. It is a really hard thing to accept, though, because when you make an amazing friend, there's no thought in your mind that that person isn't going to be there for your whole life and be there to celebrate your successes and your milestones. You don't enter a friendship thinking that person is going to be temporary. But whether a friendship breaks down dramatically or you just naturally grow apart, you have to accept that sometimes life can take you down separate paths.

None of us can predict where our lives will take us – everyone's so different and we're not going stay the same forever. That means the person who might have been a good friend to you when you were 15 might not necessarily still be when you're 23. You might no longer have the same morals, for example, or the same approach to life.

A lot of romantic relationships don't work out because when you're with someone for so long, you may naturally just grow into different people. And it's the same with friendships: sometimes we just have to accept we've grown apart, value the good memories we shared, and wish them well.

GETTING COMFORTABLE WITH BEING ALONE

Knowing that you are OK on your own means that if a friendship does end, you've got the space to let it go: you're not frantically trying to hold on because you're worried about being lonely. And over the years, I have got very comfortable with my own company.

Being an influencer may look social – all those events! – but that's not the full story. Like anyone who's self-employed, you're not in an office environment where you have colleagues who are doing the same thing: you're on your own journey. And not many people can relate to your path, because it's an unusual and really a very new job to have. In my case, I'm so lucky that I've got people around me that I really, really trust and lean on. But the truth is, I also just like working mostly alone as well.

Still, it was a big adjustment when, after first moving to Manchester, I found myself alone all the time – I'd say 23 hours of the day. Sometimes I'd sit there on my sofa, thinking, *Oh my God, I'm such a chatty person, and I've not actually opened my mouth to even speak to one person today, because I've been by myself all day!* I had to become very OK with being alone, even though I do like being around people. But again – and I think this is down to my non-sociable side – I didn't really care. I didn't get lonely. And, in time, I actually quite enjoyed it.

If you are thinking about living alone and have the means to do so, I encourage you to try it. But even if you're not able to, I think it's so important to do things that force you to be more independent and happy with your own company. Because you have to be enough company for yourself before you meet a guy or girl or let whoever else into your life. What if that guy or girl were ever to leave you?

I think you have to get secure with the idea of being alone, because when it's all stripped back ... you really only have yourself, so you have to get comfortable with that.

One tip that I always give to people who are living by themselves for the first time is: play music. I did that all day, every day, and it really gave me a sense of comfort. I didn't even have a TV in my apartment when I lived alone – I just had my computer – so I'd have Drake on repeat non-stop. Or I'd play YouTube videos – shopping hauls, anything at all – just to break that silence. I think that really helped me, because silence is what can really kill the mood and your energy when you live alone – it's a bit tiring, in a weird way.

I don't think I'd necessarily want to live alone again, even if I wasn't with Tommy – but I still love being by myself. Even now, I'll always take time out to go to places by myself. I'll take myself shopping in town for hours, or even just head to the supermarket for some solo time. Living alone definitely made me love my own company and become very comfortable having days by myself.

LOVE
LESSONS

I've never really been a girl that gets guys. I never really knew how to flirt or chat to guys or anything like that. I've not necessarily struggled with it, but I was more of an awkward girl; I didn't know how to be with guys or what to say. When I was younger, my friends at school were mostly the same – we weren't really looked at by guys. So, I wasn't one of the girls who was always going out with boys and going on dates.

I remember there was a bit of judgement around that at school, people calling girls frigid if they hadn't done stuff with a boy by the time they were 16. I definitely was in that category of being called frigid. Because it just petrified me – the thought of kissing a boy or, you know, being with a boy like *that*. It was just something that I didn't start to think about until I was a bit older. Now, I think that judgement around what you have or haven't done is horrendous.

That pressure to do things with boys or else be called frigid if you don't? It's so scary.

If you're not ready, you're just not ready. And it's not cool to call anyone names around that.

When Instagram came into play, I started to get a bit more attention from boys, because in my school I probably had the most followers even if I wasn't necessarily the most popular girl. It was kind of intriguing to some people, and guys seemed to start to like me a bit because of that – which is really superficial and stupid! – but I guess that was when I started to get more male attention. So, I was always the girl that never had a boyfriend, never really got guys, and then in the last year of school, I got a boyfriend and was with him for about two to three years.

Obviously, we've all been there: we've all had our first kiss and we've all had our first time. For me, my first boyfriend was my first time for everything. I was really lucky because that relationship sort of taught me everything I needed to know, and I never really had to go through that scary (for me, anyway!) phase where you go out and meet guys and get up to mischief; I wasn't doing things with guys I didn't know. I didn't experiment with guys growing up. It was more that I met this boy, and I was with him, and that helped me understand guys. Over time, I definitely just grew out of that relationship, and we broke up when I was about 17. That relationship did teach me a lot, though, and I'm grateful for that. He had a really amazing family, too, who helped me through my parents' divorce.

After that, I just went back to being single. I dated a bit but nothing that serious, until I got into my next relationship … on national TV!

YOU DON'T ALWAYS KNOW AT FIRST

When I first saw Tommy, I found him really, really attractive. I always say to him now, as cringey as it sounds, that if I were to sketch out my dream man, I'd draw him (that is, if I could draw!) because I feel like everyone has a type and he's mine. I've always fancied guys who look the way he looks: tan, tall and muscly, with dark hair, nice teeth and beautiful eyes. He's just everything I had dreamed about in terms of what my future husband might be like. But to be honest, at the time I thought, *This guy is going to be an idiot, he's just going to be a mess-around guy.* And he just couldn't be further from that. Actually, he wasn't very good at *chat-up* chat; he wasn't particularly smooth with it.

For a while, I didn't know if there would be anything between us. I thought, *He's got the look and he's funny, but is there something more serious there?* It's also hard to pinpoint how you're feeling while you're on the show, because it's not a usual situation to be in. *Am I feeling this way because of this environment? Or would I feel the same way outside, too?*

Obviously, I know now that he was quite nervous and didn't really know how to approach things and didn't really know what to say. And when I realised that about Tommy, I started to see him for him: he wasn't pretending, he wasn't trying to chat me up; it was actually about having a natural, flowing conversation. And that's when I began to really like him. So, it was an instant attraction, but it wasn't an instant emotional connection; that grew more gradually as we got past that awkward stage of trying to chase each other. When we became friends and started to get to know each other properly, our feelings sort of blossomed between us.

Another thing that I found hard to come to terms with was that the guys I'd been with before him – and my stereotypical type in terms of personality, as I said on the show – were bad guys. Guys that don't reply to you for days on end. Guys that give you the chase and you chase them, and it's almost like a bit of a game. Guys that mess you around and cheat on you. Tommy wasn't like that at all. He was very cards on the table: *I really like you and want to be with you.*

I felt, *Oh gosh, I'm not used to this. I'm used to guys messing me around, to the point where I'll want to be with them* because *they don't want me.* I think never having been treated so kindly before actually left me a bit confused by the fact that Tommy was so into me! But, of course, I came to love how direct and open he was, and appreciate that so much – because you don't find that all guys are like that.

*I always say they don't make them
like Tommy anymore, because he has
a very old-fashioned way about him.*

Being raised as a Traveller – he's half-Traveller, from his dad's side
– his morals and values are more traditional. To him, when you
meet a woman that you love, that's your woman. You don't ever
look in another direction. You don't ever do anything that would
upset her or hurt her. It's about loyalty, through and through. And
that's just something that you don't come across in every guy.

If I had to describe what he's really like, I'd just say he's very
normal, but hilarious. I don't think anyone realises how funny he
is. Sometimes *he* doesn't realise how funny he is when he comes
out with his one-liners! He's just very humble and grounded and
kind; he's a very normal boy that has a very not-normal life, and
nothing will ever change him. I just say he's like the Big Friendly
Giant – not at all how you'd expect.

Openness in our relationship is key. To the point where some
may say we're too open – I'll even go to the toilet when he's in the
same bathroom, soaking in the tub! There are really no boundaries
in our relationship. We've never hidden anything from each other,
and that for me is something that is so important: never feeling I
have to hide my true self around my guy or be a lady around him.
That's just not me.

And I love his generosity – not in terms of materialistic things,
but in terms of the fact that, every single week, without fail, he

buys me flowers. He's just got that really old-school, romantic, gentlemanly side about him. And I think that's what Tommy has learned from the Traveller culture – how to be a gentleman – because Travellers are raised with these incredible family- and husband-material values. Every week, I get home and there'll be a card and flowers, and I know even when we're 80 he'll still do that because it's just been instilled in him.

HOW YOU KNOW

I always say you know you're in a good relationship when you go to bed at night and you get excited to wake up the next day to spend time with that person. Me and Tommy, before we go to bed, we're always having such a laugh that when we go to sleep, I think, *Oh, we have to go to sleep? I want to carry on chatting, I want to carry on laughing!* And that's when you know you're in a good relationship – because there are constantly things to talk about.

WHY I'M HAPPIER IN A RELATIONSHIP (AND THAT'S OK)

I've definitely realised over the last five years that me in a relationship and me single are two very different people. I always say to Fran, 'I don't think you'd like the Molly-Mae that was single because my priorities were just all over the place.' I'd definitely prioritise the wrong thing. Because I wasn't that good with guys – or I didn't feel I was – I'd always be thinking about what I was saying, how I was coming across, what I looked like, how I acted. Was I being cool enough?

For me, it's a case of, when you're in a stable relationship that makes you feel fulfilled and happy, you don't have to think about those things. You can put your brainpower into all the things that do matter to you – in my case, work and setting up a future for myself. You're not sat there, thinking about whether or not a guy is online on WhatsApp! It's so toxic and unnecessary.

It can sometimes feel like you're either a girl that is or isn't like that: either you just crack up guys and you're great and you're really cool with it all, or you're like me and you're an overthinker and you can prioritise all the wrong things. Which is why I'm so, so glad that I got that single phase out of my system when I was more of a teenager because now, I can be in my relationship and sort out all the things I actually want to focus on. Of course, it's totally fine if you *don't* want to be in a relationship – the thing is to know yourself and recognise what works for you.

Personally, I'm grateful that I've found my relationship now, that I'm in it in this part of my life, because it's been such an important stage for me. To have Tommy by my side has meant having that consistency and that constant reassurance when I'm going on big jobs and doing new things where I don't really have a clue what I'm doing. If I were single going through all that, I'd be juggling so many things and wouldn't know who was genuine or who to talk to. That's why having Tommy has been just so key for me and so incredible.

We both had this huge life change at exactly the same time, so we went through it together, and that was really helpful.

It's definitely made our relationship stronger, too, that we can relate to each other's lives so much. Even now, Tommy and I talk about things that happened when we first came out of *Love Island* – photo shoots that we were on, interviews that we did, red carpet events – and we'll both cry laughing at the things that we went through when we had no clue what we were doing. For example, you'll be going down a red carpet being asked questions about an event and how you're feeling, and if you're not used to it, it's so much pressure. And it's so nice to have someone that has no idea what they're doing either, so that you can laugh about it together if you mess it up.

After we came out of the show, Tommy and I lived in my really small apartment in Manchester for a little while before we rented our own apartment just down the road from there, in a different part of the Northern Quarter. But he still loves that first apartment; he's always talking about how he'd love to go back to it and see what it's like now, because that was the background to some of our very first memories together. Honest to God, the whole apartment was tiny – he barely fitted in it! – but it was just cute. Plus, that was when we really got to know each other in the outside world, and it was a really nice time to be there.

And, instead of going back to a boyfriend who has no idea how that feels and having to explain, 'This is how I felt tonight …', I could just say to Tommy, 'Oh my God …!' and not have to spell it all out. It has been so nice to be able to relate to someone in that way and experience things with them that are new to them, too. It's comforting. So, we're both very lucky that we've had each other going through it all. I've been able to lean on him, and he's leaned on me. We have strengths in different areas, in that he finds some things easy to go through, and others I find easier. We've just balanced each other out so well.

LEARNING TO COMPROMISE

I told Tommy I loved him in *Love Island* – but realistically, we'd only known each other for a few weeks. I felt like it was love then, but I only really started to know I loved him when I was out of *Love Island* and realised, *Actually,* this *is true love.* I don't know if there was one single moment; it was more something that grew as time went on.

Coming out of the show, there were so many things that we had to deal with that we'd never had to worry about before. I remember thinking, *Oh gosh, OK – it's not like* Love Island *and we're not in a dream world here. It's a normal relationship now, with normal things to deal with, with normal struggles, with normal stresses. We're not in a villa – this is real life.*

For example, when we met, Tommy already had a blue tick – he was Instagram official – and he had about 40,000 followers on there already. His boxing career had just started and he was always on the scene with his brother Tyson, who of course is really well known as a heavyweight champion. Being a Fury, you're kind of just known anyway! But he wasn't as into Instagram as I was, and he didn't always understand why I posted all the photos that I did.

Now, I would never change what I do for a guy – that was something my mum's always drilled into me: that you do what you want to do! And Tommy wasn't asking me to do that, anyway. So, I just explained that it's about showing all the different aspects of my lifestyle. He's used to it now and he's really understanding.

That doesn't mean you have to feel exactly the same away about everything. He's still more private than me. He definitely will say to me, 'Oh, just put phones away tonight' or 'Let's just go out without phones.' He really does value that time without phones, because for him social media is more something that he does as part of his boxing career, whereas for me, it's my passion as well as a big part of my business. So, he doesn't share a lot. He really does not care at all what people think about him, which is actually a really good thing for me because I can sometimes care too much. Together, we have a nice balance.

So, those early months were all about adapting very quickly and learning what our normal, outside-world relationship was going to be like, and I think we were just so lucky that it formed into what it did – and that it was even better. But we did learn how to be with each other in certain situations. He's got very specific ways that he deals with things, and I've got very specific ways that I deal with things – and you only learn about those as a couple over time.

MY RELATIONSHIP FEARS

Early on in our relationship, I posted a video on my YouTube where we answered questions. Watching that video back now, I can see that was when we were really in our honeymoon phase – the way we were looking at each other, we were just googly-eyed for each other. I was always a bit fearful then, wondering, *Will this honeymoon phase run its course one day?* Now, we're in our real relationship, where it's still so amazing. Our relationship is so real – we've definitely had our get-to-know-each-other phase, we have a routine – and yet, I've realised that the honeymoon phase never really ended.

We even got through lockdown really well. I actually loved that time with him. We're usually both so busy that I cherished getting to spend every single day together. It maybe gave us more time to spend on our relationship: learning more about each other and really getting to know each other even better – we had nothing else to do! It was just me and him and a TV. We really just sat most nights in front of a new horror film. (We're lucky that we both love them, as that's something that we really bond over.)

Still, I admit, I do get scared. Because my parents got divorced and I know it's so common these days for relationships not to work, I'm always fearful. What if, for some reason, he wants to leave me one day, or stops loving me? Deep down, I know that's about me and nothing to do with Tommy. Everyone has their own worries and insecurities, even in the best relationships. The important thing is not to let that spoil what you've got: to recognise when the anxiety is coming from you and that it's not about who you're with.

One thing I don't worry about is other girls. I think how you feel about your boyfriend or your girlfriend getting a lot of attention from the opposite sex is all dependent on how they react to it. I'm so lucky that Tommy has not changed and has really stayed so grounded, especially with having girls flocking around him on PAs (personal appearances). The fact that he doesn't do anything about it has made me realise it's OK that girls fancy my boyfriend. It's OK that everyone knows him – because I know that he's just this normal boy who tells me that he only has eyes for me. In our relationship, the key thing for us is our loyalty to each other: it's what we base everything on.

And, since he decided that I was the girl for him, he's never even flicked his eyes in another direction. I always go back to this one time, when we were in a spa together, and this unbelievable girl walked in with this blonde hair, great bum and legs – she was just stunning. You'd fully expect your boyfriend or the guy you're seeing to be having a little look. I wouldn't have even cared, because even I was checking her out! But Tommy wasn't bothered – his eyes were just on me.

I feel like he doesn't have eyes for anyone other than me and that is just the most comforting feeling.

Again, I think that's because of the way he's been raised. When you meet a woman, when you're a Traveller, that is your woman and you do not look in another direction. And it's just the most comforting feeling, being with the person you love and knowing they'll only ever have eyes for you, no matter what happens. I've been with guys who definitely didn't make me feel like that, and it's horrendous. It's just not worth your time.

So, it doesn't bother me that other girls fancy him. Also, I think all girls know that you kind of want a guy that keeps you on your toes a little bit (even if that's just in that other girls want him!). I think, *I'm that girl that gets to have you as my boyfriend – and that makes me feel so lucky.* He doesn't realise how amazing he is. And he doesn't even think he's good-looking!

DON'T WASTE TIME

I think my parents' divorce taught me the importance of finding the right person, because it does break my heart a little bit when I think of my mum spending 25 years of her life with the wrong man for her. We only have one life – every day is so precious, let alone 25 years. That's like a massive chunk of her life that now she looks back on, and it was with the wrong man.

That terrifies me, the idea of spending even one year with the wrong man. That's a year of your life that you're never going to get back. That's why, with Tommy, I had to be so sure of him before we made it serious. But I quickly realised that he was just different to anybody I'd ever met. Now I've been with him a massive part of my adult life, and it just feels so right. You just know when you've met someone that it just feels right with. So, I think this relationship has really reinforced for me that if it's not the right person, don't waste your time.

And I don't think a relationship should feel like work. I think if you have to put work into it, that's not a relationship; that's a chore! For me anyway. I think you should only be in a relationship if it adds to your life effortlessly – and it's completely effortless with Tommy. We share a bed every single night, we wake up together, we live in the same house; he gets up and cracks on with his day, I get up and I crack on with mine. And then we have a day off! We bicker, of course – that's normal – but he adds to my life. And I always say to my friends, if they're ever with a guy that doesn't add anything to their life, then they have to get rid – because why waste time when you could be finding the right guy that just makes you feel amazing every day?

Having said that, it's important that people know we're a very normal couple and do have arguments. I think people sometimes assume that relationships they see on social media are just absolutely perfect all the time. Tommy really is what girls would call a 'goals' boyfriend! But every single relationship has conflict, and we can bicker like cats and dogs. I often talk about the reality on my

YouTube: if I'm filming a vlog, I'll say, 'Oh my God, Tommy and I have just spoken about something, he's really annoying me today.' I'm very real about it. There are things that he does that irritate me and there are things that I do that irritate him.

But one thing about our arguments is they're literally always over in five minutes: we can't be angry or upset with each other for more than that. Afterwards, I think it's kind of nice when you've had an argument with your boyfriend, and then you make up and have a hug – you almost love them even more because for that one minute, you hated each other! (Of course – and it should go without saying, but it's important – I'm talking about normal, healthy conflict that you can sort out. If you're in a relationship that's more arguments than not, or if it's making you unhappy, then honestly, don't put up with that.)

GROWING TOGETHER

Tommy and I are very similar in many ways. We have a lot of the same interests (we're both obsessed with horror films, for instance, and we both love Halloween – October is our favourite month of the year), plus we're the same age. With him and I, everything just fits. I always say that we're like two peas in a pod, because we do almost everything together – especially because of how small my circle is as well.

It does feel like we're an old married couple now. I always say to him, 'I know you better than you know yourself.' I feel like I know how his brain works, to the point where if he's ever in a bad mood, the only person that can talk him out of it is me just because I know him so well, and he can do the same with me. And I will often say something before he's even said it, because I know he's about to say it.

But we do appreciate each other's differences, and we both have our freedom, too; when he has to go off for the day or for a week, or if I do, we just get on with it. It's never a case of complaining, 'Oh, why'd you have to go away?' We just accept it. Then, when we get back together, it's great: we appreciate each other more. I think when you spend time apart you can actually learn just how much you love that person and how much you love spending time with them.

Since we've been together, Tommy's become much more mature. I think he's definitely turned from a boy into a man – he's just become an even better version of himself.

If I hadn't found Tommy, I think I'd be single for sure. With my career what it is now, I don't think I'd have time to meet someone. I'm just so lucky that now, living with him, I don't have to make a conscious effort to spend time with my partner – if we're not with each other all day, it's fine; we'll see each other at the end of it! It happens naturally.

But more importantly, I don't think anyone else would understand my job, whereas he gets it. We have very different paths:

he wants to be a world champion one day, and I want to have an incredible business and do amazing things in the fashion industry. They're so different, but we build each other up. He takes my Instagram pictures for me a lot when I need him to, and I always come to training with him to watch him. We just really back each other.

We share goals for the future, too: we both want kids relatively soon and that is really because when you're with someone and it feels so right, the next stage you see is having kids with them. The thought of him being the father to my kids one day makes me so beyond excited – it's just the most amazing thought in the world for me. So, I think we have so much to look forward to and we can't wait to get engaged and get married; we talk about it literally every day. He's such a family man. We both do have a lot of fun, and obviously, we both go away a lot separately, but we're settled in our relationship and just really lucky to have found each other.

Still, there's no rush! For the time being, we're happy with the children we do have ... all 17 of them! We call them our children, but really, they're our collection of cuddly toys: stuffed giraffes, turtles and more. Ellie Belly is my elephant, who's literally been with me since I was a baby and who I took into the villa, and all the others have names, too ... but there are 17, so I'm not gonna list them all!

And we do believe that they come alive when we're not there. OK, we'll act like they do, anyway. So, when we go out, we'll leave the TV on for them and a bag of crisps next to them. When we've been to places like the Maldives and Dubai, we've even taken a duffel bag specifically for the 17 children, because we cannot leave them behind. One time, we nearly missed our flight to Dubai because one went missing. We would not leave until we had all of them together, because the thought of leaving one of them in the living room by himself made us want to cry.

Which goes to show, when you find the right person, you're not worrying about whether they think you're cool or not – you're too busy having fun with them.

MY ADVICE IF YOU WANT A RELATIONSHIP

Stop looking for it.

I always say that the reason I did find love when I went on TV was because I knew I wasn't going to feel deflated if I didn't find love. It was more a situation where I felt like I had nothing to lose. Tommy and I were the only people that year who ended up in a relationship, which is ironic – and everyone who went on there looking for something didn't find anything.

But I feel maybe it happened for me because I wasn't intentionally looking for it. Like I said, there were other reasons I wanted to go on the show. I saw it as a fun opportunity. Tommy was the same: he had a break between fights so, when he was approached by ITV, he thought, *Summer in the sun? Can't go wrong!* And I think because of that, because I went in looking for nothing, I found him.

The minute you just take the pressure off
and stop looking for someone,
that's when it happens.

TOMMY'S TAKE

Tommy: *'I knew that Molly was the one for me – and I'm not just saying it – when I met her in the hot tub on* Love Island. *When I first laid my eyes on her, I thought,* Yep, she'll do for me just fine! *And I soon knew that she's everything that I would want in a girl. She's absolutely stunning inside* and out, *and that's very important. Molly is very hardworking, very intelligent, a massive people person – always putting other people before herself – and very loving, very thoughtful. When I'm having a bad day, she just knows how to pick me up and says all the right things. She's always there to help and is just an all-around great person.*

'What people don't realise about Molly, and one thing that I'd like to share, is that she is also absolutely hilarious. She's not just this hardworking, intelligent influencer, she's extremely funny – and that's one of the main reasons that we have such a good relationship and are as strong as we are. So it's definitely a good trait of hers!

'But what I like most about our relationship is, no matter how busy we both are, whether we're in different parts of the

world, we can always come back together and have our time –
there's a time for work, and a time for us. And it's amazing to
see that, no matter how busy we both are, we still make that
time for each other: we go for long walks on the weekend and,
at the end of the day, when we get in bed, it's just us. We still
get our time, which is very important.

'And if we do go away, it's always absolutely amazing and we
always have the best time – wherever we are – because we're with
each other. Every time we're reminiscing in bed, going through
the pictures and videos on our phones, it's always to do with
our holidays,. 'Do you remember going here? Do you remember
doing this, or that?' They're the most special times for us.

'In the future, I'd love to see us get married and start a
family together. I want about four to six children, but I think
Molly only wants one – so I've got some working to do there!
But that's definitely what I'd like the future to hold for us: a
nice marriage and to start a family, me and her. That's what I'd
want out of our relationship. So, God willing, everything keeps
going like it's going, 100% that's definitely coming …'

FACING
THE TRUTH

MY BEAUTY
JOURNEY

Growing up, my favourite magazine was *Mizz*, which was a bit like a kids' *Cosmopolitan*. When I was about 11, I saw that you could enter a competition to win a photo shoot and be featured in a two-page spread in the magazine. For a while when I was younger, I really wanted to be a model – yet another dream of mine – so to enter, I made a little booklet of photos with a quote on it about why they should pick me. I ended up winning and having a full photo shoot printed in the magazine, which I could take into school and show everybody – which, of course, I loved!

Those pictures look quite funny now because at the time I had extremely short dark hair – I'm not a natural blonde! I'd always wanted to cut my hair short, but my mum had never let me, until finally I went into the hairdresser and asked for a 'Frankie from The Saturdays' look, which meant I ended up with hair long on one side and cut short on the other. I just thought she was so cool to have such a different look, so I thought, *Yeah, I'll go for the same!*

Eventually, Frankie got the long side trimmed the same length as the short side ... so I got that as well. By this point, I had hair almost the same length as Tommy's now. It was so short – horrendous on me, really! I actually put a picture of it on my Instagram Stories and people were so shocked to see me with this short dark hair; it wasn't even a bob – it was not my favourite look. Of course, I loved it for about two weeks and then I hated it, exactly as my mum said I would. Mum had told me, 'Don't do it. You're not gonna like it.' But I did it anyway!

After that, I spent about two years watching 'how to grow your hair naturally' videos on YouTube, learning what I could put on my hair in terms of different oils, home remedies and products to help it along. Luckily, my hair grows quite fast, but it was not a good stage. I don't know why I thought I could pull off Frankie's haircut when I was a kid with no clue how to style it! It was a really silly thing to do, but everything's part of the learning curve.

So, not all of my beauty adventures have been total successes – but it didn't really matter. In fact, I think that's probably why the magazine picked me as the winner: because not many girls my age would have had that kind of hair at that time. I had 'cool' hair that was a bit different for a young kid – and that's exactly why I'd wanted to have it cut like that, so that people would be saying, 'Did you see that? Molly-Mae had her hair cut like that!' I always wanted everyone to be talking about what I was doing, so having my hair cut short was just another way to achieve that.

In a way, it's lucky I was like that, because it wasn't just dodgy haircuts I was dealing with. As my dad mentioned earlier, I was born with a big strawberry birthmark on my forehead, which might have bothered some people growing up. For a long while, I didn't want to get rid of it. I wanted to keep it because – again! – I actually liked having something about me that was a bit different and made me stand out from the other kids.

As I was heading towards secondary school, my parents thought maybe it was time to get it removed, because they didn't want me to get bullied or anything like that – I don't think I was very aware of how kids could be. Luckily, I hadn't had any problems with anyone teasing me about it, I think because I was confident about it. It wasn't an insecurity of mine at all – which, looking back now, is perhaps surprising, because the birthmark really was noticeable; it was raised and bright red. If I had been much older, I think I would have been upset about it, but at the time I just wasn't. Still, my parents encouraged me to maybe think about getting it removed, so eventually I did, and it's left just a tiny scar on my forehead that's very faint.

My parents have since told me that when I was little, other adults would often stare at me because of my birthmark, which of course they didn't like. That's why, on occasion, when I've noticed a child with a strawberry birthmark like mine, I'll go over to chat to their parents if the moment seems right, just to reassure them: 'I had a birthmark exactly the same as your baby's and as I got older, it shrank and lost its colour. Then I had it removed and now I've just got this little scar.' It's not that I think the parents care about a birthmark – mine didn't – but I know they can worry for their child, because when you're so little and innocent you have no idea that you've got something different about you that people could be mean about. Thankfully, I didn't really realise when I was younger that some people might think that my birthmark affected my looks. I just didn't care!

OFF DUTY AND ON

There is still a big part of me that doesn't really worry about how I look. For instance, I only wear make-up when I have to. Every single day I have off, when I'm not making content, I'm in wet hair, with no make-up. I love dressing down, I love tracksuits and comfortable clothes. That's another reason why I hate nights out: because I hate putting on high heels and a dress where you have to hold in your breath all night, then you go out and girls are looking at you, guys are looking at you … it's too much! I literally love to be at home with a hoodie on and just relaxing. If I didn't have the job I do, I'd wear gym clothes and no make-up every day.

*I really appreciate the days where
I don't have to do my hair or
make-up and can dress comfy.*

I still have a love for it – don't get me wrong – but because it's now my job, when I don't have to work, I don't want to put on make-up. In the same way, when I worked at the gym, I lost my love of exercise a bit because working out became, well, just work. I've lately felt like I've lost my love for doing my face for an evening out. I spend a lot of my time glammed up for photo shoots, so when I get my chance to I love using different skincare to feel fresh-faced.

It's hard, too, having to look a certain way all the time. That's a pressure that I do feel sometimes: because my work involves having to look good and take pictures and wear nice outfits, it's almost like modelling, at times. Maybe you don't look like you've made an effort when you're wearing no make-up, but sometimes I actually feel better without it – it's just nice, isn't it, to be able to rub your face?! Sometimes it's just nice to not have to worry about the things you'd worry about while doing your job, which for me involves make-up and hair. Sometimes you just want to have a spot on your cheek, not try to conceal it, and just sit there and eat chocolate and not be that influencer!

And if I can get away with it, I won't wear make-up on my grid. I really do love to do no-make-up pictures, like when I'm on holiday, for example. People like to see a bit of everything – full glam, but also make-up-free. As long as you switch it up now and then, people stay interested. That's why I always change up the backgrounds of my pictures and shoot them in different locations, in different cities and towns and countries, because that's what keeps people engaged with your life: what are you doing next? Where are you going next? But it's much, much harder to shoot an Instagram picture without make-up, just because the camera can really wash you out – you just need a little bit of something on your face. I know Instagram so well and I know what works for me.

The pictures I post on Instagram are the highlights of my life – the good part of my day – and I hope that's clear to my followers. What you see on Instagram is not what life is like 100 per cent of the time.

It's probably worth saying here that, in the society that we're in now, pretty much most influencers and girls do edit their pictures. And I'm not going to sit here and say I don't edit my pictures because I do – but I don't edit them to alter my appearance. I'll never change my body or my size. There are apps where you can, say, change the tone of the photo and brighten it up, to make the colours pop, so I'll use those – and I've been very transparent about it.

I've made videos on YouTube about how I edit my Instagram pictures, and I'll show the stages from start to finish, in terms of how I remove things from the background or add a filter or sharpen a photo. It's enhancing what's already there. And I make that very clear on my socials: that the way I edit is more to make the picture look better as a whole. It's not to fundamentally change or warp the way I look. Because if you want to see the way I look outside of a photo, you can just go over to my YouTube and watch me live! You can't filter YouTube at all.

I think that's why my audience are very trusting of me, because if they want to see a more off-duty version of me, everything's there for them to see, completely unfiltered and completely raw, even first thing in the morning when I wake up and I'll be vlogging and haven't brushed my teeth or brushed my hair! I think it's nice to show those two sides: the YouTube side, where it's more relaxed, and the Instagram side, where it's glossier.

And I've always been very transparent that when you see someone's Instagram pictures, you're seeing just one snippet of that person that they've chosen to give you. While I do think my Instagram's a good representation of how I look in that moment, no one looks the way they do on Instagram all the time – it's just not the way it is! For 90 per cent of my life, I'm literally in pyjamas or something just as comfy, with no make-up on, hair in a bun. So people need to remember that Instagram is not real life. It's literally what that person is choosing to put out; and, let's be real, not everyone's going to want to put out a picture of themselves having a bad day or not looking their best.

It's just like a highlight reel – the best parts of everyone's lives. On my YouTube, I always say, 'Take Instagram with a pinch of salt – it may look like I just nipped out to grab a quick Starbucks, but it may have taken me 100 tries to get that picture! But it's my job to show the outfit that I'm wearing and show you guys what I'm up to.' So, enjoy what you see on Instagram – I do! – but just remember it's not always what it seems.

BLONDE AND BLONDER

I've always had a massive interest in hair. I enjoy doing my own and, as I mentioned, I used to work at a hairdresser's when I was 14. Because I'm quite a girly girl, I used to watch hair tutorials all the time on YouTube: how to curl your hair, how to put it in a protective bun ... and, after I cut my hair short and it was the biggest regret of my life, how to grow it more quickly!

So maybe it wasn't a surprise that I dyed my hair for the first time when I was 15. I did it behind my mum's back, tried to dye it blonde and then had to tell my mum when it had all gone tits up and I needed her help to fix it.

I had always wanted to be blonde, and I'd thought a box dye – the stuff you buy in a shop, rather than getting your hair done in a salon – would take me there, but that wasn't the case. The box dye was a complete disaster and I ended up with a colour that was nowhere near the bright blonde I was after. My mum was really strict with things like that – I wasn't actually allowed to dye my hair – but then obviously when I saw what had happened, I couldn't hide it: 'Oh, Mum, it's gone wrong ... Help!' In the end, I had to go to a professional hairdresser to get it fixed and finally ended up closer to the blonde shade I had been aiming for.

Before that, I had really long, thick dark hair in incredible condition, because I'd never touched it. By now, I've had blonde hair for so long that I feel like it's a bit of my identity. I don't think I'd ever change it. Still, growing up, it did mean I dyed it so much that the condition of my hair was pretty much destroyed – if you dye your hair a totally different colour, it can cause the strands to break and go thin. That's why I actually ended up having to have extensions later.

I was about 17, and it was so, so expensive. I remember my first appointment cost £900, which obviously was just ridiculous. I had to borrow my mum's money and promise, 'I'll pay you back!' I look back now and think, *What were you doing?* Back then, £900 seemed all the money in the world to me. That would have been my whole month's earnings gone. But again, I just think it was one of those things where I felt, *Well, no one else is doing this, so I'll go and get hair extensions put in* (extensions weren't as big a thing then as they are now). I added length and thickness, and that was when that addiction started.

Maybe I was rebelling a little bit by that point, too. As I said, my parents had been strict to the point that if my friends were going out to get their acrylic nails done for the summer, I was not allowed to do that. I remember so many times my friends would be going to get their nail extensions, and my mum and dad wouldn't let me: 'Over our dead bodies! You're not doing that.' But after they divorced, I definitely managed to get away with a lot more because there was only one parent to push things past. I guess I felt like I could just get away with murder … and I definitely did for a few years! The minute I could, I went a bit overboard.

It was as if I thought, *I can get away with all this stuff now, so I'm gonna go do whatever the hell I want to do!* But by doing that, I screwed myself over. Because that's how the lip fillers came about.

FALLING INTO THE FILLER TRAP

I had just turned 18 when I first started getting lip filler. It might sound surprising that I started getting treatments so young. But I was headstrong: even though my mum might tell me so many times, 'Please don't, please don't,' if I said I was going to do something, I was going to do it! I'd never been a naughty child and I like to think I was obedient. But when I look back on it, maybe I wasn't so obedient, because I was doing all these things that my mum told me not to do …

No one I knew had fillers; the area that I grew up in was quite an innocent place, a bit disconnected from things like that. No influencers would come from Hertfordshire, I thought then; it wasn't like London or Manchester, up-to-date, cool cities! And it was only through Instagram, social media and TV that I even knew about fillers. None of my friends were getting anything like that.

But I wasn't just looking at the girls I knew from school or work or fashion college. I was looking at people who were older than me, all the influencers that I followed. At the same time, I was trying to become big on Instagram myself. I started thinking, *Maybe if I get lip fillers, and cheek filler, then I'll take better pictures and I'll get more followers and I'll get more people that like me …* What I didn't know then is how that becomes a vicious circle, one you can't really get out of that easily. You end up trying to do more and more in the hopes that people will find you prettier, or cooler – and that's just not how it works. That was something that I wouldn't understand properly until later.

Back then, I read something online about a full-face package a clinic was offering: a package deal on getting filler in your lips, cheeks and jaw. That kind of thing was everywhere on Instagram; you couldn't get away from it. Even now, you can see posts about filler packages or cheek filler or non-surgical rhinoplasties – there's something for literally everything. And I think because it's so normalised, by seeing those things on Instagram, you can think that everyone's doing it. If you see an ad that suggests you can go and get a full-face package for £400 and look amazing, you might think, *Oh I'll go and do that then.* I did. When I learned about this injectables deal, I thought, *If I go and do that, I'm gonna look unreal! I really want to try it.*

Sometimes, there's a perception that only insecure people do things to their face – the truth is, I don't think I've ever really felt insecure or vulnerable! When I first got filler, I was actually feeling really confident. My followers at that point were just rocketing, and I was thinking, *Why are all these girls wanting to follow me? I must be doing something right.* It was a real confidence boost, because obviously I could have gone on Instagram, posted my pictures and nothing could have happened, but it was all taking off really quickly.

But what did prompt me to do it was that, again, I was trying to be different, to get ahead of the crowd. My friends certainly weren't doing anything like that – none of us were in a position to afford it, but me being me, I was just winging it. They all thought I was crazy, but then again, I was always doing different things to my friends at home, because of my not wanting to do the typical thing. So none of that stopped me. A lot of girls on Insta seemed to be getting filler – it was the cool thing to do – and it was just a very minor procedure, I thought, not really a big thing. I hadn't even been thinking about filler for that long before I ended up doing it. Now, of course, I know that doing anything to your face is something to be taken really seriously.

MY NOT SO LITTLE SECRET

I didn't start off with the full package – I got my lips done first. I actually had to wait a little bit to start doing them because I was still doing pageants at the time and I didn't want it to hurt my chances of winning; the organisers were really against filler. I think in the pageant world, you wouldn't have been seen as a good role model if you'd gone and got filler. So, as soon as I finished doing pageants, that's when I did it! Not long after I'd come back from China, I went up to Manchester to have it done, along with my friend I'd met through pageants and who lived up there.

I got 0.5ml of lip filler that first time, which isn't a big change, and I really liked the result. I didn't tell my mum at first. I just prayed and hoped she wouldn't notice because I knew she'd be really upset. But eventually, I ended up telling her anyway, because we have such a good relationship – we have no secrets. 'Mum ... I've got lip filler,' I told her. She was actually quite nice about it. 'Oh, it doesn't look bad,' she said. 'If you'd told me you were going to get it, I would have imagined you'd end up with big blow-up doll lips!' And it wasn't like that at all. It was a tiny little change to my face at that stage.

But I didn't stop there. In fact, before I went away to try a season in Ibiza, I had 1ml of filler put into my lips at one time, which was too much given that I already had some in there – that was a ridiculous thing to do! But because I was planning to go away for months, I wanted to get loads in because I thought I wouldn't be able to get it done again for a while. Afterwards, my lips were bulging – they looked like they were about to burst. Soon, my face wasn't looking better, it was actually just looking worse – especially when I started getting jaw and cheek filler, too.

How that came about was, after I'd had lip filler injected two or three times, I thought, *Well, I've got my lips done – I'll go and get it done to my whole face as well.* So, I went for the full-face package – cheek filler, jaw filler and lip filler – which cost around £500. And the first time I got that done, I actually liked the way I looked. I only had a small bit of filler injected during the procedure, so it actually did what I wanted it to do and made my jaw look really sharp – I now had a right angle for a jaw. I liked it because that was what was quite in at that moment; everyone wanted to have a 'model' jawline. So, I was quite happy with it at first.

After that, I'd go maybe every six months for more. People do go for top-ups – the filler used is not classed as permanent – but I was going overboard. Looking back, it was just a downhill slope, really. I think that's my biggest regret with lip filler, that it led to me starting to put filler in different parts of my face. The lips were one thing, but I think messing around and putting filler in different parts of my face was just so dangerous. Doing that changed the way I looked completely. I looked like different people before and after I had it done.

I was in a vicious circle,
where I just kept going back
for more and more and more.

At the time, though, I didn't think like that. In fact, I decided to get something else changed, too. Three days before I left to go on *Love Island*, I went to the dentist for composite bonding. How it works is, your natural teeth stay as they are, and they put a layer of white composite material over your natural teeth to make them look perfect. And, in retrospect, that's another massive regret of mine because they looked so fake. There was literally nothing wrong with my natural teeth, but somehow, I'd convinced myself that they didn't look good.

UNDER THE MICROSCOPE

As I've found myself more in the public eye, one thing I have had to deal with is 'before-and-after' pictures – when they find old photos of you and compare them to how you look now. It's never really bothered me, but one thing I would point out is that every-one's face matures, whether or not you've had filler; your face ages.

No one's face stays the same from 16 to 20! So even if I hadn't had filler, those before-and-after pictures would still be out there and people would say, 'Oh, you've had this done and this done.' People are convinced I've had a nose job … and I haven't. But people always want to say that you've had these things done. I didn't really mind that when it first happened, and I still don't.

That's not to say I haven't got upset about what people say about photos of me, though. Coming out of *Love Island*, I went to get my filler done again and opted for another full-face package of jaw, cheek and lip fillers. That was the big one! I remember the girl that did it was injecting 2ml of filler here, 2ml of filler there, 1ml of filler in my lips. In other words, I had loads. How much did I have altogether? God knows.

After having that load of filler done when I first came out of Love Island, *I haven't actually had filler again since.*

Soon after that, I filmed an outro to a YouTube video. I'd just gone to LA for a massive shoot with PrettyLittleThing and needed to film the last part of my vlog, where I said goodbye, so I just turned on my camera quickly to record a quick message: 'Thanks for watching, guys, see you soon, bye!' But because I'd had all that filler injected the day before, my face was just so sore and swollen that it looked honestly horrendous. Someone took a screenshot from that video, and it just went viral. That picture of me looking so swollen literally went everywhere, and everyone was talking about it: 'What's Molly done to her face?'

I was more embarrassed than anything, because I never wanted to be that girl that was known for having a face full of filler. I didn't necessarily judge other girls for that – I'd be thinking more, *Oh God, what's she done? She didn't need to do that.* But I realised that somehow, I'd become that girl without even noticing it. I was just more mortified than anything that people were looking at me as that unnatural, face-full-of-filler girl, and I just hated it. But still, I told myself it looked fine, that it would go down, it was just the swelling.

So, for a while, I just kept hoping that my fillers would just settle down in time. I didn't realise, at first, that the only way I was going to go back to looking how I wanted was if I actually dissolved them. I was still not 100 per cent accepting that they just didn't look good. I'd tell myself, *I'm being self-conscious – it* does *look good. I didn't get this to make myself look bad. It has to look better, I definitely look better than I did before …*

It took me really a long while to realise that my face didn't look better, that actually it looked worse than when I started with it all. My once-sharp jawline was looking more like jowls, sort of hanging underneath. My lips felt lumpy, uneven and unnatural. Over time, I had got a bit more, and then a bit more, and now they didn't look right.

Of course, by this point my swollen face had been made fun of everywhere online – it was trending on social media and being made into memes – while I had been trolled quite badly. On one level, I didn't want the trolls to think they had 'won' if I reversed what I had done to my face. I think I was also scared that dissolver wasn't going to work and that there was no way to undo what I'd done. But eventually I admitted to myself, *This just doesn't look right – this just isn't me.*

I felt less confident, more than anything. I didn't feel prettier. I didn't feel better. Actually, filler had just made me feel worse.

The final push I needed came when I was out at a PA Tommy was doing. While I was waiting for him, I sent my sister a selfie. The shape of my face in this photo looked so bad: distorted and unnatural. I remember sending her a message saying, 'Oh my God, look at my face. I'm gonna have to do something about this.'

Thankfully, Zoe is the one person who is always so, so honest with me. 'I agree,' she replied. 'I think you do need to do something about it.' Finally, I booked in to get my filler dissolved.

GETTING REAL

I was so scared when I went for my first dissolver appointment, in early 2020. Because I had so much filler in my face, I was thinking, *This isn't going to go anywhere, this is going to be here forever.* But when the dissolver was injected, my jaw went from swollen-looking to completely back to normal again in about 10 seconds flat. The minute the product hits the filler, it just *goes.* Basically, the body naturally breaks filler down over time, but injecting this dissolver does something similar in seconds, not months.

Afterwards, I looked in the mirror and I automatically felt like me again – and it was just the best feeling in the world. I hadn't even realised how much it had been affecting me, how it was making me feel so self-conscious, having all this filler in my face. It's supposed to be something you do to make yourself feel better, but by the end I was feeling horrendous. The minute I got my filler dissolved, I was so happy.

*Thank God, the minute the dissolver
was injected, the filler just disappeared,
and my face was back to normal again.
It was the best feeling in the world.*

It was my jaw and cheek filler that I had dissolved first – the lips I left for a while because, again, I didn't think they looked bad. They took me a bit more time to get to – another year or so – because I wasn't ready to let go of them. I didn't have the same regrets about my lips; I actually liked the way they looked and they didn't bother me. But after some time, since everything else was going natural, I just felt like my big lips could go as well. I really couldn't picture how I'd look without them, but when the dissolver went in, they flattened instantly and were back to how they'd been before.

It took me a good few weeks to get used to them again. When you've become so accustomed to the way you look with all that lip filler, then suddenly go back to how you looked before, it feels weird at first. To be honest, I was mortified; I felt like I had literally no lips. But then I got used to them again, and then they started to look normal to me. That's another thing I'm now really glad I did.

At first, I didn't want to talk about the fact that I'd had my jaw and cheek filler removed, because I didn't want to admit to people that I'd made a mistake. I didn't want people to know that I'd realised I'd messed up! I remember thinking, *I hate the fact that people are gonna think that I'm weak and that I can't stand by my decisions.* So I just didn't speak about it. I didn't want anyone to know.

Then when I had my lip filler dissolved, I couldn't keep doing that, since my lips went from really big to absolutely nothing! So I just decided to be honest and talk about it. And in doing that, I realised how important that was: a lot of people will speak about everything else related to filler, but not a lot of people admit to feeling like they've made a mistake with it. I even put up a video about me getting my lip filler removed, which got a lot of views. I think a lot of people just wanted to see what I looked like without any lip filler! But I think others were genuinely interested to see the process and what was involved. In my case, I had to have three appointments altogether to get everything out – two for my face, one for my lips – and I went to a few different people to do so. There are so many practitioners out there who are really good at reversing mistakes.

Honestly, I feel like that's what a lot of them are known for these days. Filler was so popular a few years ago, and now it feels like a lot of people are trying to reverse what they've done. That's why it's such a blessing that my filler was reversible. If it wasn't, I would literally have destroyed my face. (But it's worth remembering that doctors say even procedures that aren't supposed to be permanent can have serious, lasting effects, so please always do your research if you're considering having anything done.)

I really didn't expect the reaction that removing my filler would get. A lot of people were tweeting about what I'd done, saying, 'Seeing Molly-Mae do that made me realise that I actually don't need my filler. I'm going to try to get mine dissolved.' I also had so many messages from parents, saying this was such a positive thing to be able to show their daughters and to teach young girls that getting filler isn't necessary. It was a surprise because I didn't choose to remove my filler for anyone but myself, but I'm really proud that what I did inspired other girls to embrace their natural beauty too.

I will say that my decision to do so was about what was right for me, and I am not telling anyone else to do the same. At first, I loved the results I had with filler – it made me feel more confident and if I hadn't taken it too far, I might never have had it all reversed. And, so long as you go to someone that knows what they're doing, and you're at an age when you're allowed to do it and you can afford it financially, you might not have any issues with filler. But this is my story, and I messed up using it and eventually had to admit that and address that.

These days, I have absolutely no filler in my lips, no filler in my jaw, nothing in my cheeks. Even though I've had those appointments to dissolve it, sometimes I will feel my face and think, *I'm sure there's still a little bit in there* ... but I think it's pretty much all gone now. The only thing I've got now is a tiny bit of Botox in my forehead – that's the only thing I have done. For me, it's all about finding that right balance.

• • •

It felt so right to get rid of my filler, I eventually went back to my natural teeth, too. That was another situation where I told myself, *Just do it*. The night before my appointment, I almost cancelled! Technically, I hadn't brushed my real teeth for about two years – disgusting, I know. I was sure they were going to look awful. But, as I always do, I thought, *I want to do it, so I'm just going to do it* – and I did.

Fortunately, because the layer of composite protected my real teeth, it was fine: there was no actual damage to my natural teeth when the composite was removed. Still, it wasn't a nice feeling when I looked in the mirror for the first time. It's a bit like when you have your hair extensions removed; no one else will even notice it but you, but when you're used to your 'perfect' hair and you go back to the old, real version, it looks rubbish. And my teeth did look pretty horrible and yellow at first, because obviously they'd not been touched for two years. I remember telling people, 'Don't look at me! No one talk to me!'

But really, I was lucky that my natural teeth were still intact. With veneers, which people sometimes go for to get that bright white look, the dentist grinds the tooth enamel away, so if I had opted for that, it would have been irreversible. After I'd had a bit of time to get used to my natural look again, I was just happy I had any teeth left. Now, I just whiten them, and I feel so much better. I can now see I looked so fake before.

All in all, I feel as if in two years I had aged myself about 10 years. And then, when I had all these things reversed, I felt like a younger me – I looked my age again, which was such a good feeling.

The whole experience of reversing my cosmetic procedures has really been life-changing because it's taught me how to be happy in my own skin. Even though I was almost resistant to it at first, and scared that I would look bad, making the decision to be more natural has forced me to be comfortable with myself and my body, the way it was intended to be. It was a learning process – one that took time – but ultimately it was a path I'm so glad I followed.

HOW I'VE EMBRACED BEING MORE NATURAL

Looking back now at my younger self – at that girl who had all that work done – I'd just say it's sad, really, really sad. There are pictures of me that I really struggle to look at these days, where I'm so filled that I look like somebody else. And it's so sad that I felt like that was beautiful and that was what I needed to do to be liked and to be desired.

I wasn't doing it for myself. I was almost doing it for other people, to get more respect and to be more liked.

It also feels sad to me that so many girls out there are hoping, like I did, to be prettier, looking at other girls and wanting to look just like them. Even these days, I know I look at celebrities and think, *I wish I looked like her.* But then I remember that some girls probably look at me and wish the same, while there will be girls, in turn, that look at them in the same way … You always want what you don't have! Back then, that was me: trying to achieve the same look as the girls who I thought were stunning and beautiful, and hoping that other girls would then feel that way about me. But actually, if anything, what I was doing just made me look worse.

I don't necessarily know if I really would change anything I've done, as I've learned a lot – and I try to share what I've learned with other girls, too. I'd like to think that what I'm doing now is setting a good example to girls and showing them that you really, really don't need to do the stuff that I did. In documenting how I got my old teeth back, and how I got rid of my lip, cheek and jaw fillers – really stripping it all back – I wanted to show that it's OK to make mistakes when you're younger. But that, when you grow up, you're only going to realise you shouldn't have done those things!

It's like when you get a tattoo or a piercing – just remember that in five years' time, you might not want that tattoo, that piercing … or those lip fillers. That's why you should wait and be patient and, yes, listen to your mum, listen to your dad, listen to the people around you (like me!) that have made those mistakes already.

Now, I do think young girls wanting cosmetic injections should really be turned away. The technicians should be telling them, 'Have you really thought about this? Wait a few years for your face to mature.' In fact, they have now made that the law for teenagers: if you're under 18, you can't be injected with Botox or filler in England if it's for a cosmetic purpose. When I did it, I didn't even need to bring ID, which I think is worrying. There was no question of being turned away; I just had to pay, sign and get it done – it was the most straightforward thing. What happened wasn't the fault of anyone injecting me – I just didn't know where to stop. But some places won't advise you that they don't think you need something done. Whereas the places I go to now, for a small amount of Botox or whatever, they will actually say to me, 'You don't need to do that.' They're not just about making money.

When I look back now, it just makes me cringe that I felt at that age, I needed to do all that.

My fear is that, if I'm lucky enough to have a daughter one day, she would want to do something similar, and I wouldn't be able to convince her otherwise. I just hope and pray that she would listen to my advice when I say, 'I've been there, I've done it, I've got the T-shirt. And trust me, when you're older, you'll regret doing that!' Of course, you always think you know best. I definitely didn't listen to my mum – she could have screamed from the rooftops that I didn't need to change my face! But I hope my pictures will show girls that it's not a good idea. Filler isn't necessarily a bad thing in itself, and I know, for some people, treatments can help them feel more confident, amazing even (although I would *always* say make sure you go to someone professional with a good reputation). But there's a definite line – and when you've hit that line, you have to stop there, and I didn't. Even though people were telling me to, I just didn't.

The problem was I was so not ready and so not informed. I wish I had taken it all much more slowly, that I hadn't rushed to get injections in my face, to get bigger lips and bigger cheeks. Because there was plenty of time; I didn't realise it then, but you have so many years to do those things. And if you wait, you might find you don't want to do them at all …

So, if a young girl told me she wanted a full-face package – or whatever else was on offer – I would just tell her to wait. Wait just a few more years, until you know it's something that you definitely, definitely want. Do your research. But most of all, stop trying to be something that you're not. Remember, the way you're born is completely perfect and individual. You don't need to try to look like anyone else, because you're not that person. You are you.

I know I'm not the only person that felt the way I did, so it scares me that other young girls will be feeling the same, and probably doing the things that I did. As cliché as it sounds, I wish I'd accepted then that I was beautiful the way I was.

FINDING BODY CONFIDENCE

A CHANGE
IN LIFESTYLE

Growing up, how my body looked just wasn't something I worried about in any way. As a family, we ate healthy food, but I never thought about what I was eating. I'd eat what I wanted. I think mums always get concerned food will be an issue for their daughters, especially when growing up. Mine was always asking, 'What are you eating today?' to check I was getting all the nutrition I needed as such an active kid. But, for me, it really was never an issue.

Only when I got a little bit older did I become more aware of that type of stuff. It's sad that when you hit 14 or 15, a lot of girls start to think, *Oh, maybe I shouldn't have all that chocolate, maybe I shouldn't have all those sweets.* That was when I started to become more aware of my body and to think of how it maybe 'should' be looking. That's also when I was heavily into Instagram and really finding my feet on there. And obviously, I'd be looking at these huge influencers, like Kylie Jenner, and all these girls with these incredible bodies. Still – and maybe it's because I was so active – my body image wasn't really a problem for me.

That did change, sadly. When I came out of *Love Island*, I really lost my love for fitness over the following year, and I gained a bit of weight. As a result, in the last few years, my face isn't the only way my looks have been criticised. My body has come under fire, too, and I have definitely battled with my body image.

For a long time, as life got busy, I didn't have time to think about anything other than just work and setting myself up. So, for a while, I just put healthy eating and exercise to the back of my mind, and I really did lose my way around that for the first year after the show. The gym, exercising and being active, and doing things other than just working and relaxing, or going on date nights with Tommy and stuff, became such a non-priority to me. I had PAs every single night for a few months, and photo shoots around the world, which meant jet lag (so I wasn't full of energy for exercise). When you're travelling, it's also a case of grabbing what food you can, when you can. I was literally having WHSmith meal deals from a service station at three in the morning because that's just what fitted in with my schedule.

I really didn't realise that my body actually wasn't going to deal with that very well. Looking back, I was sort of in denial, thinking, *Oh, I'll be fine if I have spag bol every single meal for a whole week.* I was getting spag bol for my dinner and putting chips in it, and just having whatever I could! But the reality is, I'm not that person. I have to keep on top of exercise and my diet to stay in a shape that I'm happy with and I feel confident in. I think I gained about two stone during that period, from when I went on *Love Island* to after the first year out. So, I had definitely prioritised different things.

For a while I did try to find a way of balancing socialising and going out for work events and dinners with keeping on top of my health. I'd find myself in these weird periods of crash dieting, going to these mad, really hard gym classes I just couldn't do, and just trying everything I could to feel more confident within myself. I wanted to feel like the old me but live this new lifestyle … and I couldn't really find that balance.

I come from such a sporty background as well, which is why I think everyone was quite worried about me. My parents have raised me to be very aware of how to look after your body – you're only given one body and you have to take care of it. And for that first year, I definitely didn't. My family, especially my sister, told me, 'You really need to get back into it.' Just because my family is so, so sporty, and they knew that fitness had been such a huge part of my life.

But they were talking to me about it because they were concerned about my well-being. Meanwhile, other people were about to notice too – and they didn't really care how I felt at all.

ONE BAD PHOTO
AND A LOT OF TROLLS

Towards the end of 2019, I'd gone to Barbados with my team on a trip for my new tan brand, Filter by Molly-Mae. It was a huge campaign shoot, because I was going to be launching the brand with the images we took, so I was really focused on that. Barbados is a tiny island, and everywhere we went was lovely quiet beaches with no one there, let alone any paparazzi around – or so we thought. I think that's why we were surprised by what happened.

We were outside, shooting photos of me in a white bikini, when I remember seeing a man taking pictures of the building behind me. What I would realise later is that he was pretending: he was actually taking pictures of *me*. Soon, they were all over the *Daily Mail* website … and I felt like they were just the most horrendous images of me.

At the time that set of photos came out, I definitely had changed physically. I wouldn't say I'd 'let myself go' (which was what some people said, and much worse). But I think the petite size 6 Molly everyone saw on *Love Island* had morphed into more like a size 10 Molly-Mae – which was still perfectly fine! And, oh my God, it's crazy that I have to say that – but it wasn't what people were used to seeing me looking like in a bikini.

The headline they used was 'Molly-Mae Hague displays her curves in a TINY white bikini.' With pieces like that, the papers almost use a bit of sarcasm – so they write a headline that almost reads like you think that of yourself. It will say something like, 'Molly-Mae flaunts toned stomach', and then below that will be a picture of you looking completely bloated with not one bit of ab definition on you! I just couldn't believe it, and of course the photos went viral.

Some people might justify photos like that by saying that they are 'real' – but actually, they are not necessarily any more real than a picture you might see on Instagram. I've got pictures of me in my bikini from that day, completely raw, unfiltered, unedited, and I don't look anything like the pictures that they published of me. Even if you scrolled down to read the rest of the article, there were better pictures included that I was fine with. But of course, they didn't use one of those as the main image. because that's not what sells the article and makes people want to click on it. A picture of me looking like I've got rolls and belly fat is what sells – and they'll stick in a picture from my Instagram, so it looks like I've photoshopped that.

And at the end of the day, I know the paparazzi are just trying to earn a living. The problem is they don't have to deal with how that feels; they're just the ones taking the pictures. They're not that girl that has to face the fallout. I look back now at that poor 20-year-old girl, reading vile comments about her being fat and how she needed to lose weight, and comments about 50-year-old women looking better than she did at 20 (and I'm not saying that women can't look great at 50, of course not! But that's not what the commenters were suggesting). People just don't understand how that can affect someone. Luckily for me, I am fairly strong – but it did really upset me at the time.

We had just flown back to London when the pictures came out, and I remember ringing Fran, crying and saying, 'I'm gonna ring the *Daily Mail* myself!' I had this idea that I could ask them to take the photos down. Of course, she was telling me it wasn't a good idea, but I told her, 'I'm doing it now!' And I did. I just rang a customer service number at the *Daily Mail* and got through to a receptionist or someone like that. I was sobbing my eyes out, saying, 'This is Molly-Mae Hague and I'm ringing to say you need to take those pictures down!' I'd lost my mind over this. For me, it was genuinely a nightmare come to life. So, that was not a good day!

Needless to say, the pictures stayed up online. I can actually laugh about that dramatic phone call now, but I really was teary for days afterwards and just wanted to hide myself away.

HOW I PLAYED THE PAPARAZZI

I did turn the tables on the paparazzi, in the end. Not long ago, we were shooting a campaign in Ibiza, again for my tanning brand, Filter by Molly-Mae, and of course the last campaign that we shot in Barbados had been leaked to the press because of the paps. With this trip, we wanted to keep the campaign extremely under wraps and not have anyone know we were shooting before it went live.

Around midday, we stopped for some lunch at Formentera, an island just near Ibiza. The paparazzi spotted us and I decided we couldn't let them follow us, ruining our exclusive campaign. So instead, when we realised the paparazzi were following our boat, we went down into the hold with one of the models, Emily, who had blonde hair like me.

The paps had seen me in a restaurant earlier that day, so we put her in the same dress I'd been wearing, did her hair the same as mine, put my sunglasses on her, and even my bag. Then she sailed away on a smaller dingy so that the paparazzi followed, taking photos of her instead. So the switch worked – it was really funny. It was all over the press that I'd swapped boats and so on – little did they know that this wasn't actually me!

WHY MY BIKINI PIC BACKLASH SCARES ME

Mainly, when I think of the trolling I get, even now, it relates to my pictures – especially bikini photos – and the comments on articles like the one about the pap shots in Barbados. For any girl, any woman – any human, really – to be torn apart for how you look is something that is so, so hard to come to terms with. It's so difficult to sit there and say to yourself, *Just ignore it.* Because when someone's saying they don't like the way you look, it's so hard not to look in the mirror and think, *Are they right? Am I ugly? Am I fat? Should I lose weight?*

There were a lot of things that played a part in me changing my appearance since then – and a bit of me doesn't want to admit that the criticism affected me – but, honestly, I think the comments calling me overweight did have an impact. I realised

I hadn't been taking care of myself and, afterwards, I did start prioritising my health again. But no one should ever have to face that kind of criticism, that damage to their self-confidence, just because their body has changed. It's so concerning how when I was a bit bigger, I was called 'fat' and 'obese'. The fact that a size 10 is deemed 'lardy' and 'overweight' is just petrifying. And that's not even the point: all sizes should be accepted in exactly the same way. No one deserves to be called nasty names for how their body looks. All bodies are beautiful.

Reading the comments under articles like that actually makes me more fearful for other girls my age who might see the comments written about me and think, *I'm actually bigger than Molly-Mae in those pictures … So, if she's been called lardy there, well, what am I then?* Not only does that nastiness affect me, but it's also going to affect thousands of other girls, because it's almost been made OK to say things like that about me at that size. It makes me scared for other girls because if I'm not being accepted as a size 10, then maybe they're not feeling accepted as a size 10 either – or whatever size they may be.

The words that get thrown around now about girls' bodies are just not right. It's actually dangerous.

MY TRICK TO DEALING WITH BAD PHOTOS

Nowadays, I wouldn't react to photos I didn't like in the same way I did to those ones from Barbados – but I'm not going to pretend they don't bother me at all. If I see a bad photo of myself, straight away, I start to wonder what other people might think of me when they see it. And my initial thought of what they might write is sometimes 'Molly-Mae looks fat', just because of the bad experiences I've had in the past with the articles and comments.

Of course, the reality is that when you're standing up, posing for an Instagram photo, with your make-up on and your hair done and wearing a flattering outfit, you're not going to look the same as you would when caught completely off guard, sat at the swimming pool with your belly rolls on show – because, let's be real, every single person's got those! Still, not everybody is caught on camera that way and then has the pictures splashed all over the place. But when you're feeling vulnerable, you might think, *Oh God, am I the only person that looks like that in a bikini?*

Maybe it's not an entirely positive thing to do – maybe the best thing would be to totally ignore them! – but if I see photos taken of me that I don't like, I'll just scroll through my Instagram feed. Because I think it's very easy to look at a bad picture of yourself and think, *God, is that actually what I look like?* Obviously, it's a photo of you and that's what you look like in that moment. But angles, lighting, everything can make such a huge difference – and that goes for any photos you don't like of yourself, too! Just remember that that's just one picture. That's just one angle. That's just one type of lighting. It's not any more 'real' than all the lovely photos of you.

HOW I FOUND
MYSELF AGAIN

Finding my way back to myself, and figuring out a balance that works for me in terms of looking after my body, wasn't an overnight process. After those pictures from Barbados came out, I started thinking a bit more in terms of *I want to exercise, I want to get back to my routine.* But it wasn't that simple. If I thought Barbados was a wake-up call, there were a few more to come. On about four different occasions, in fact – every time pap pictures of me would come out that I didn't like – I would say, 'Right! Now's the time that I'm going to make a change.' And I'd make a small change and I'd start exercising again, but it wasn't really working for me.

I was trying loads of different things. I was getting personal trainers on board – I must have tried five different personal trainers – but something wasn't clicking, and I think it was because mentally

I wasn't ready to go back to the gym yet. Meanwhile, I wasn't eating healthily at home. So, I was seeing no results and getting pretty disheartened, then I'd give up again. It was a battle, and I wasn't getting anywhere with it.

I was just really unhappy with how I felt in my body. By then, I had my tanning brand out, Filter by Molly-Mae, and everyone was asking me to show my routine, in terms of how I apply my fake tan. But I was never able to do that for my followers because, at the time, I didn't feel able to be open and honest about the way my body looked. The last time people had seen me in a bikini, on TV, was very different to how I looked a year on. So, I was kind of hiding myself a little bit.

It got to a point where Tommy and I went on a holiday to the Maldives, in December 2020, and I realised, *I've actually really messed up here. I'm really, really not prioritising things that should have always been a priority, not just because of the way I look, but more importantly for my health – including my mental health.* It was a real turning point for me.

The difference then, though, compared to when I'd seen those Barbados pictures and felt so bad, is that this was a realisation that I'd reached by myself, for myself. There were no paps in the Maldives – we'd gone there for a bit of an escape.

This time, it wasn't about what other people thought of my body, it was about how I felt.

And I realised a few things about myself that holiday: that I had just lost myself a bit, and I just felt like crap, really. That's when I had the true wake-up call and came back from holiday wanting to make a real difference. For me, it got to the point where I was like, *I need to do something about this now.* It was definitely a step that needed to be taken.

A FORMULA
THAT WORKS

So, it's only been since around the start of 2021 that I've made the biggest changes and lost the weight that I put on. And now, after getting back on top of my health, as well as after having all the cosmetic work undone, I just feel like a different person.

In the end, what worked for me was really just not putting pressure on myself to exercise every single day. I did it really slowly and built it back up again. Sometimes I'd go to the gym, and I'd stand on the treadmill, do a little walk … and that'd be it. But I used to say to myself, 'Well, it's better than nothing – last year you would have done nothing.' So, for me, the formula that worked was not applying too much pressure and just letting myself gradually fall back in love with exercising.

I didn't go on a diet – it was just about making healthier choices and getting back to the old me, because I've always been a very healthy person; I've always liked to make healthy choices when I go out, but I struggled to do that in the first year after the show.

My lifestyle had changed completely in that time, and it took me a while to find a way to balance everything properly.

And I didn't hire a personal trainer. I've always had female PTs and I think sometimes I felt … not jealous, but a bit of pressure, because obviously they had their fitness journey together because they were personal trainers, and they were smashing it. And I just felt anxiety going into those training sessions because I had become so afraid of the gym and now had to go exercise with someone that really knew their stuff. So, I simply took that pressure away by doing what I could by myself, with no one shouting at me or telling me what to do. That really changed my perspective on exercise. I would go and do what I could, and then I'd go again and do a little bit more, and then the next time I'd do a little bit more again. That was a much more positive way for me to go about it.

The lockdowns actually helped, too. I know that wasn't the case for a lot of people, and I can totally understand why. But before the pandemic, Tommy and I had a bad habit of going out for food a lot. (Definitely for the first year we lived together, we ate out pretty much every other day – if not every day. We lived above a restaurant that presented itself as offering healthy food, but it wasn't really. We'd go down there every single day and order roast dinners, you name it!)

Then, because of lockdown, obviously all the restaurants shut, and we were cooking for ourselves much more regularly, which actually did help. And with everything just calming down and me having more time to focus on the things that make me happy and make me feel good as a person, I could come up with a plan as to how to get myself in better shape.

MY ROUTINE TODAY

At the moment, I go to the gym about four times a week – it's easy living with Tommy because he trains three times a day, so I just go along with him. We do try to exercise separately once we're in there – mostly because he gets annoyed by the fact I don't know what I'm doing! But he does help me out; he's really good with stuff like that.

I love the stepping machine, so I will spend a bit of time on that, and then I'll go on the treadmill for an incline walk – so nothing too hard. I love cardio. I can go to the gym and do 30 minutes of cardio and I'll walk out, thinking, *I'm glad I did that – I feel better for it. It's not loads. I've probably not done that much or worked out as hard as I could have, but it's better than nothing.*

And I have tried to introduce weights a little bit recently. But it's quite daunting, isn't it, when you go into a gym and you don't really know what you're doing? Especially now that some people know who I am. I hate the idea of people telling their friends later, 'Oh, I saw that Molly-Mae last week. She hadn't got a clue what she was doing in the weights section.' I'd be mortified! So, I normally put a YouTube video on my phone, and headphones in, and follow a little ab workout or something like that. The one thing I'm terrible at is home workouts. I cannot do them to save my life – I just get distracted. I switch the TV to something else or get my phone out.

You do feel like a different person when you come out of the gym. After a session, you just feel so proud of yourself and happy that you did that, especially since, for me, it's been a journey of trying to fall back in love with exercise. Whenever I have a good session now, it gives me a real feeling of accomplishment. Remembering where I was compared to where I am now, I feel like, mentally, exercise has put me in such a better place. You just feel more positive, and things don't feel like a chore. Even walking to places doesn't feel like an effort anymore – your health, your fitness, is that much better. Everything just improves.

Really, there's not one negative thing about exercise. OK, the only negative is that you sometimes can't be bothered to go, and it can be painful and tiring and you get out of breath! But the feeling you get afterwards just trumps any bad feelings before that, really.

Since I've been exercising again,
I'm a different person. I feel so much
better in every aspect of my life.

MY ADVICE ON GETTING OUT OF A (NO) FITNESS RUT

If you've fallen out of love with the gym, like I did – or maybe even the thought of going gives you anxiety – just go and do what you can. Set yourself mini goals and then, every time you go to the gym, try to do a little bit more. It's about not being hard on yourself: if you go and have a bad session, it's OK! It's actually fine to go to the gym and not do anything that taxing. At least you made the effort to get up and go. And it's better than what you may have done the day before – it's all about building it up.

THE WAY I EAT

Now, I'm really in a good place with my relationship with food and eating as well as exercise. The one thing I want to say is that this is the way of eating that works for me – what works for you might be totally different, and that's fine.

The first thing I think about when I wake up is food. I've always been such a breakfast person. I normally get up, then make myself a protein shake; that's something that has really helped me to get on track – finding a breakfast that works for me – because it starts your day right. Before that, if I had an unhealthy breakfast, I'd think, *Well, I've had that breakfast, I'll just have whatever else I want for the rest of the day.* When I started introducing protein shakes for breakfast, that really helped me make healthier choices. Everyone laughs at me now, because every single place I go – whether it's for an overnight trip or a one-day shoot – I'll take my blender with me and everything I need to make my shake. I'm so adamant about having my protein shake for breakfast, just because it always sets me up right for the day.

For the rest of our meals, Tommy and I really don't do that much cooking just because we don't have time. Whenever we used to do a big grocery shop, all the food in the fridge ended up going off, which is so bad. Besides, because his diet is so strict before a fight, it's just not that easy to get all the macros right and get everything measured.

So, we decided to stop doing that and just eat when we needed to eat. He'll use a meal-prep service when he's in camp, which is when he's training ahead of a fight (sometimes boxers do go away for camp, but he'll usually stay based at home, confusingly). He works with a meal-prep company, so his meals are delivered to him every week to keep in the fridge and microwave when he wants one. Sometimes I'll have one with him, but a lot of the time I'm out, so I'll just make healthy choices: I'll grab a salad or soup for lunch and something a bit more substantial for dinner.

Then, when Tommy's out of camp, he'll just eat whatever the hell he wants: curry for breakfast, Chinese for lunch, pizza for dinner – he goes in! I think because he's so restricted when he's in camp, he just tries to scoff it all when he's out. I have had to have a few chats with him to explain, 'You can just eat what you eat, and I'll eat what I eat because we're very different.' He's training all the time for his job, and I'm not!

I've still got a real sweet tooth, though. I always crave something sweet, so if I'm grabbing a snack, I love a protein bar. It is basically a chocolate bar – it actually probably has more sugar – but I think, *Ooh, I've had a protein bar!* And I'm obsessed with Quavers: my number-one snack is a packet of Quavers, while my treat meal is spag bol. When Tommy's organised a date night, he's even had private chefs come round to cook us an unreal spag bol, because he knows that that's my favourite. So, for me, it's all about making healthier choices where I can, but still enjoying myself.

WAKE-UP CALLS

Recently, I have had a couple of scares that have really underlined the importance of looking after myself – reminding me that, more than anything, it's your health that really matters, not what other people think of how you look.

It all started when I noticed a mole on the back of my leg. It came up about two years before I went on *Love Island*: a really small, bright red mole on the back of my calf. And my mum noticed it too – 'Oh, that's weird' – but it wasn't growing, and it was just small. It looked a bit like my strawberry birthmark, so I wondered if it might be that. It was harmless, I thought.

Then, when I went on *Love Island*, my mum actually rang up the show and said, 'I can see this mole on the back of her leg, and it looks like it's got so much bigger since she was home.' She thought maybe being in the sun had caused it to grow, or maybe she'd not noticed that it had changed until she saw it on-screen. As she said, 'I shouldn't be able to see it on the TV if it was as small as I remember it.'

So, while I was on the show, they were checking it every four days – they had a medical team who were measuring the mole with a tape measure to make sure it hadn't grown, and they were really good with that. They'd call me aside, measure it, note it down, check it hadn't grown. But then, when I came out, I forgot about it for about six months – life got so busy. Again, my mum was worried, saying, 'Get it checked, get it checked.' But I'd say, 'No, that's just not a priority right now. I know it's fine.' But eventually, I thought I should really get it checked again.

Still, when I went to the doctor's, they said it was nothing to worry about. In fact, I had two or three doctor's appointments where they said to me it was nothing to worry about. So, I forgot about it again. I said to my mum, 'It's nothing to worry about, they said it's fine.'

Then, in 2020, I happened to go to the doctor's about something completely different. As I was leaving that appointment, I remembered: 'Oh, just one more thing: can you just check this mole on the back of my leg? I've been told it's nothing to worry about – I just want to be reassured one more time.'

She took one look and said, 'That needs to come off right away. I can tell that's not an innocent little mole, that needs to come off.' Afterwards, I remember coming back from the doctor's, sat in the back of an Uber. For a second I had this realisation that this could be life-threatening. *Is this going to be serious?* I wondered. In that moment I had so many uncertain thoughts and it really put my health into perspective.

Within two days, I was having the mole removed at the Christie Hospital, a specialist cancer hospital in Manchester. What they do is send it for a biopsy – testing. I was on a Beauty Works shoot in Venice when the doctor called me to say, 'It's cancerous, a malignant melanoma. So, you'll need to come back next week and have the skin on your leg around the mole removed and biopsied.' They explained that I had to have the biopsy to make sure that what they thought was cancer hadn't spread; while removing the skin around the mole was to create almost a safe margin around it – so they knew they had removed all the cancerous cells. It was a lot.

Ahead of my further surgery, I was isolating, as Covid restrictions required at the time. But then, three days before I was due to go in, they rang me to say, 'We're just not sure what this mole is – within the clinic, we just can't decide. We just really don't want to remove the skin on your leg unless we have to.' So instead, they sent the tissue off to New York, where it would be checked by a team of senior expert dermatologists to try to work out what it was. I just had to wait for any news, which was horrible. My mum was so worried, of course: 'Have you heard anything? OK. Anything else?' And all I could say was no, no, no.

Finally, after a month of waiting, the surgeon rang me again. 'We just want to leave it and we don't think it's a melanoma.'

I couldn't believe it! I was saying, 'You cannot do this – I've literally been told I've got a melanoma. How am I meant to relax now, knowing that?'

But that was the end of it. The doctors just said it was nothing to worry about. 'We made a mistake. We thought it was a melanoma, but it isn't.' And you have to trust them, I guess.

Now, I've just got a small mark on my leg from having the mole removed, whereas if they'd had to operate further it would have left a much bigger scar. But that experience shaped me in ways that are less visible. Hearing someone say the words 'it's cancerous' was such a massive wake-up call for me. I told myself, *You really need to start prioritising your health more because if something happened tomorrow, you could get so unwell and everything you've worked for could just disappear.*

Before that, I was so not focused on anything other than just trying to scrabble my way through my new life and my new relationship. There were so many things going on that I wasn't even worrying about my health or anything that seemed a bit wrong with my body. But now I've got much more focus on that side of things.

I realised that you have to prioritise your health, because if you don't, what are you actually working for?

That whole experience also made me much more aware of my body. Recently, I found a lump in my left boob; the doctors checked it, and it was benign – not cancerous – but they still wanted to remove it as it was growing. And I feel like if I hadn't had that mole scare, I wouldn't be so aware of everything going on with my body. At the same time, I had a lump that was on my finger removed too, just to be safe. (I feel like it's been one thing after another with my health, but I'm grateful to be happy and well now.) So, now I think that was a bit of a blessing that I had that first scare, because it made me prioritise different things and it made me value the important things so much more.

MY HIDDEN HEALTH CONDITION

I've started talking about another of my health issues, too. In October 2021, I had keyhole surgery to treat my endometriosis, a condition where (and I'm going to repeat the NHS definition to be totally clear!) 'tissue similar to the lining of the womb starts to grow in other places, such as the ovaries and fallopian tubes'. The main symptoms include period pain that keeps you from doing your normal activities, pain during or after sex, and heavy periods.

It was a really long process to get to that point. In my case, I had really painful periods for about five years – so, so long – but other issues related to my endometriosis only developed once I started seeing Tommy. Before I was with him, I wasn't really having sex, so I didn't really think there were any problems other than my period pains. But then when I was in a relationship and just became really aware of that side of my body, I thought, *There are so many things wrong – something's not right.*

I was suffering horrendous pain – literally feeling like I'd been stabbed in the stomach, just awful – and it was causing me so many issues. Big TMI! But my sex life just became non-existent: it was not a part of our relationship. The pain was affecting my work, too: Fran knew not to book in certain things when I was due my period because the pain was like nothing I'd experienced before – I knew it was just not normal. Sometimes I've had to take off a full week of work, it was so extreme.

*I can see why so many girls want
endometriosis to be talked about
more, because it's just awful.*

But it took a long time to find out what was causing all this. Over the years, I had so many check-ups with so many different doctors where I was constantly being told, 'Oh, it's this, it's that, it's thrush' – everything under the sun, except what it really was. 'Try not using shower gel, try different underwear.' I just thought, *No, it's not that. I know it's not that.* I just knew myself.

Finally, in the summer of 2021, I went to see a specialist at Wilmslow Hospital, who told me, 'You do have endometriosis and what you've been going through isn't normal. Don't feel like you're being dramatic – it's just not normal.'

I thought, *Thank God someone is telling me that.* It was such a relief to finally hear, 'You have endometriosis', and not to be told that I was having normal period pains or was being dramatic about it or that there was nothing wrong with me. That diagnosis explained everything, and I went in for keyhole surgery to treat it.

Basically, they burned away the endometriosis cells on my cervix, which is at the opening of your womb. (Apparently, the affected cells are really obvious; for instance, when you look at someone's cervix, they're like little black cells. I've googled it so much now!) As it was keyhole, the surgery wasn't major – although I did have a general anaesthetic, the one that sends you to sleep – but hopefully it will make a massive difference to me over time.

The surgery itself went well. The doctor actually took loads of pictures showing me the endometriosis cells, which were really interesting to see. But it was harder to recover from than I thought it was going to be – I was in a bit of a mess afterwards. Literally, my stomach was the size of a beach ball and I could barely walk, I could barely stand up, so it was pretty tough, and it took me about a week to recover.

A girl had commented on my Stories about a photo shoot I did a few days after the operation, for Filter by Molly-Mae for Black Friday, saying it was unrealistic for me to set standards like that for other girls suffering from endometriosis; that I shouldn't be promoting going back to work so soon. I replied to her, saying, 'Look, everybody's journey is different and everyone's individual recovery is also different. I'm not telling anybody that they need to go back to work straight away. I had a photo shoot that week where I wasn't due to be working but I felt well enough to work so chose to do so. Everyone's recovery time and circumstances are all different, and for mine I felt comfortable to do my job without feeling like I was pushing myself, so it felt OK to do that.' Of course, someone else's experience might be totally different to mine.

If you have endometriosis, I can't promise surgery will cure everything. I'm going to have more check-ups, because I still have issues related to the condition and my periods are very painful. But, the difference is that I can get on with my day, whereas before if I was out somewhere and got my period I would often have to go straight home, as I wouldn't be able to stand up. Now, the period pain has subsided to the point where I can finish what I'm doing, then drive home and manage it with the right painkillers. So, over-all, the treatment has helped.

Endometriosis can also affect fertility, and Tommy and I want to have a baby soon, so it was really important to me that I get it sorted. I was pleased to hear the operating doctor say that I have a healthy womb and everything's looking OK in that respect, for when I do try to have children. But if you do have it – or think you might have it – please don't panic, because there is help out there. As a first step, talk to your GP or visit endometriosis-uk.org.

In the meantime, I want to keep talking about it because it can be a really painful condition to live with and yet it's not really spoken about very much. Since I've started sharing what I've been suffering, so many girls have said to me, 'Thank God, I feel like I can relate to you even more now, because I have suffered this for so long, too.' They really want me to help educate people on it properly, which is something I want to do, too.

TRUE CONFIDENCE

Where I'm at now is the most confident I've felt, 100 per cent – now that I've reversed everything I'd had done, got back on top of my fitness, and everything is pretty much back to the way it was before. Which is ironic, really, because you try all these things, as I've said, to make yourself look better.

Dad, Zoe and I were always active
and adventurous growing up.
We had so much fun.

I remember my grandparents telling me off
for the above crimped hair!

I always tried out different hairstyles, even back then ...

Some early shots from fashion school in London. Feeling super grown up.

I went into my Instagram archive to find some of my early influencer posts for you. I thought I was really grown up at the time but seeing them now I look so young!

mollymae
Covent Garden London

View Insights

Boo[st]

Liked by debgordonx and **780 others**

mollymae Best afternoon with @prettylittlething

PrettyLittleThing and Beauty Works were really here from the early days!

mollymae

View Insights

Boost Post

Liked by stephanielamx and **18,921 others**

mollymae Sunday's$_{zz}$^{z} Head to my story to see how I create these curls using the @beauty_worksonline professional styler. Code 'MOLLY10'. #beautyworks ad

... look how far we've come! This was the day I announced
my position as Creative Director at PrettyLittleThing.

These are some of my favourite images of me and Tommy. I can't wait to see what the future holds for both of us. On to the next chapter ...

*But actually, in the end, all I wanted
was just to go back to how I was before
I did any of that stuff to myself.*

At the same time, I have learned a lot about how important it is to look after your body – that your health is what matters, and anything else is just secondary. It's been a journey, a process of trial and error, of learning what makes me feel worse and what makes me feel better, and of trying to get my lifestyle right. Now that I've got to where I am, I feel like I've learned from my mistakes and found out what works for me.

I ended up celebrating this moment in a really special way, too: when *Cosmopolitan* magazine asked me to be the cover girl and face of their summer 2021 double issue. This wasn't just a huge career opportunity for me, but a personal milestone: it was the first magazine shoot I'd done after having everything changed – since dissolving all my filler. It felt huge. I barely wore any make-up on that shoot because they wanted the look to feel really fresh. I also didn't have any control over the image that they chose, which, looking back, was probably a good thing because it makes you try new things and look a bit different.

Of course, me being me, and my worst critic, when I first saw the picture they'd chosen for the cover, I hated it. I told Fran, 'I will not post that anywhere. No, nobody can see that!' But when the magazine came out, people really loved it. They were actually telling me, 'Oh my God, you look incredible, this is the best you've ever looked – you look so much better now.' When I saw everyone's reaction, that was a real confidence boost. We all need some kind of reassurance every now and then and it feels great when people compliment the way you look. After making changes, it was really good to have people saying to me, 'You look better for it.' Now, I look at that cover picture and think, *That was different … which is interesting … which is good!* In fact, I really love it.

But the changes I've made aren't just about how I look – they're to do with how I feel on the inside now, too. And the people around me can see a massive difference in me, in my attitude. I even wake up earlier in the mornings now. Tommy and I, when we lived in the centre of Manchester, we'd sometimes be ordering Deliveroo at three in the morning, and going to bed at 4am. We were living that city lifestyle, and everything was accessible at any time of day. Now, we've moved out to Cheshire, and we have a really good routine: we'll be asleep by eleven o'clock. I just don't even recognise the girl I was compared to the girl I am now. It's really changed.

Only recently, an article came out with some not great pap pictures taken of me at the hotel I was staying at for a work trip. Fran and I were about to fly home, and I was scrolling on my phone and saw them just before we took off. For a while, I actually sat there thinking that if that had happened to me a year ago, I would probably be crying on the plane. Instead – without even realising it – I have become a lot more tolerant of things like that. I know now that whatever is going to be written in the comments on some article, I've actually done really well in getting myself back into exercising and feeling healthy again. That was what I wanted to do – but even if I hadn't, that would be fine, too. Ultimately, it is just about remembering that as long as I'm happy in my body and feeling confident, why would I care what people say about me?

It sounds really cringey, but I do feel now it's all about embracing what you have, because you might as well just make the most of it! Just as I always say to myself that you only have one life, you're only given one shell to live in. So, don't hate yourself for things that aren't going to change – you just need to embrace what you have and enjoy it.

MAKING WORK WORK

THE JOB OF AN
INFLUENCER

Not a lot of people really understand what goes into my job and what I do. I think people just see me as an influencer – which, in their eyes, means I take pictures for a living and I post them. But it becomes so much more than just taking a few pictures and posting them online.

Everything has to be thought about: everything you do, everything you say and everything you post has to have so much planning and time behind it. Fran and I, we're never not on the phone to each other. We're never not texting. It's a constant conversation about what the plan is for today, what we're doing and what we've got to do to get to the next step.

So, let me explain how it all works …

MY WORKING WEEK

I'm not a morning person. I never have been. I never will be. You know when you wake up for an early-morning flight and you have a tummy ache, and your body's asking, *What are you doing to me?* You want food, but you don't want food – you're all over the place. I'm like that every morning! During the week, my days can start quite early – I might be getting up at 5am for a 7am call time (the start time) on a shoot, or have a meeting first thing, and recently I've been going to the gym for 6.30am, to fit it in. But if my schedule allows I'm not a morning exerciser; I'd prefer to go to the gym later – whenever I can, really – just for an hour.

My work really varies by what I'm doing on a given day. The days where I'm shooting for Instagram will be days that I really need to make sure I'm organised and plan, so that I can fit in the time to set up and get photos. Other days, it's more a case of what I get done in that day, I'll get done in that day! In the group chat with my management team, it's a constant conversation about what we need to do and when: every Sunday evening, the girls who work with Fran will send through a schedule for the week, and every day it will say where we need to be and what we need to get done.

When I was just influencing, 100 per cent of my week was getting content, pictures, filming YouTube content or editing my YouTube. Now, I think that part makes up around 20 per cent of my days or my week. My working week is so much more than just my content. I spend a lot of time strategising, in meetings, discussing finances, focusing on my creative director role at PLT and running my false tanning business. I oversee many things, and maybe that's a side of me that people don't see because there's so much work that goes into the behind the scenes of my platforms now. That's where Fran comes in, to make sure my schedule is organised so that I can give all the things I work on my undivided attention. I think it's important to be productive, not just busy. If you manage your time well, you can be the most productive with the time you have in the week. I feel a sense of achievement at the end of the week knowing I've done everything I can.

With that said, I still spend a lot of my working week on my socials: I'm in charge of my whole Instagram, my DMs, my YouTube – I create and edit everything and haven't handed it over to anyone else. I'm too much of a perfectionist for that! Each week, I like to spend two to three days purely catching up on content and making sure that I'm taking outfit pictures, filming YouTube videos, and really engaging with my audience – making sure they can see enough of me so they feel they know me, they can relate to me and they want to invest themselves in my life. Because that's how you build a relationship and develop loyal followers – when they feel they really know you and understand you.

But I don't just have those two or three days and then think, *That's it, that's my socials done!* I'd say five days out of seven, I'm taking content for Instagram. A lot of influencers will take all their content in one day for a whole week – they'll shoot 10 Insta images and then that'll be their week's content done. That doesn't work for me. I have to take maybe two images maximum in a day – that will be photos for two grid posts, involving two different outfits, two different looks. That's because I like to change up my hair, change my make-up, and also it just looks a lot fresher and more current if you post as you're going about your life – which my followers respond to best, as I'll explain – so I don't like backing up content.

So, if I get two posts in a day, I'm pretty happy with that. And if I get one, that's still an achievement for me. I think people just don't realise that Instagram content is not something that is super easy to create. On the simplest level, one thing I do find hard is the pressure during my week to always look nice. I love having my dress-up days but I also love wearing my Harry Potter PJs and being comfy. It's all about balance. But I'm taking pictures for my Instagram pretty much every day, so I typically do need to make an effort, do my hair and look put together so that I get the best images possible.

More traditional photo shoots, for the brands I work with or my own brand, Filter by Molly-Mae, represent another massive element of what I do. I'd say I normally do about two to three shoots a month, but then I could have some months where I won't shoot at all. It just depends what we've got on. But again, it isn't just about turning up on the day and that's it; everything needs to be planned out and prepared. For me, it starts about a month before, because I will be eating well, working out – I prep my body to feel confident in myself, so that mentally I'm in the right frame of mind. With PLT, I have a huge input into the whole shoot – locations, dates, the hair and make-up artists, and so on – so I plan it all with them. Likewise with Beauty Works I'll be checking the running of the shoot. If I'm preparing for another sort of job – say, if I'm doing a campaign with a brand – it's about doing your research so that if someone asks you a question you really have a full understanding of what you're talking about.

Another big time commitment is that I have a lot of meetings: for example, I go into PLT quite a few times a week for face-to-face meetings with the team. And then I'm on FaceTime to Fran for at least three hours every day, discussing work. I can't be in every meeting that she is, so for, say, a contract negotiation, she will discuss it with me afterwards and see what I think. If she's been talking to a brand, she might say afterwards, 'This is what we've come up with: that you do four TikToks for this brand over the next year. What do you think?'

I will have a think and might reply, 'Let's say three – because then I can set this amount of organic TikToks in between.' I'm always thinking about what my Instagram followers and other social media followers see, to make sure I get the right balance of paid content and non-paid content. I need to make sure I have enough space to post as much natural, organic non-paid content as I can so that my sponsored content never starts to feel too much for them.

That's really the most important thing for an influencer to remember: to keep posting that natural, organic content that first brought people to you. That's what makes you grow. And I think about growing every day; as an influencer, you never want to stop growing – you never want your following to plateau or decrease. At the moment, my daily new followers on Instagram average in the five figures, because of how frequently I post.

Weekdays and weekends can roll into one for me because I work from my phone, so that I can kind of pick and choose the days that I hit hard, and those I don't hit so hard. And a weekend doesn't mean

I'm not posting on Instagram: I post every day. So, on a Saturday I normally post in the morning because then if people go out in the evening, they won't miss it. And then on a Sunday, it could be in the morning or in the evening – but here's a tip: Sundays are the best day to post, because it's not such a busy day for your followers, since everyone's at home having a roast or doing whatever. That's why you'll find a lot of influencers will make big announcements or save their best content for a Sunday, because it gets the highest engagement. Monday to Thursday is usually good, but Fridays and Saturdays, when people are heading out, tend to be not the best days to post.

So, that's the overview of what a week might look like for me. But let me tell you more about what I see as key: my socials. Because every move I make on Instagram, from every single Story to every single post, is done with intent. It's about keeping the vibe chilled and relatable, but also being conscious that what I post is going to make an impression on nearly 6 million people, so it needs to be a positive one. It's a similar story with YouTube, where I now have 1.6 million subscribers. I think people just don't realise the sheer amount of organisation and thought that goes into it all!

So, let me share how it all works …

MY APPROACH TO INSTA

My Instagram is everything to me – I see it as the main strand of my business. Everything I do, from my tanning brand to my work with other brands, is shared on Instagram to let people know about it. I don't really use any other method of promotion.

Instagram, as my key platform, is also how I promote my YouTube channel. As you'll have gathered, I don't use my platforms in isolation – it's all about working them in a joined-up way. So, every time I make a new YouTube video, I'll post about it on my Instagram, which takes my followers over to my YouTube channel. And likewise, on my YouTube, I'll let them know that I have just posted something on my Instagram. I'm always using each platform to promote what I'm doing on another platform, to make sure my followers are seeing everything.

Momentum is key to being successful on Instagram. It's not a job that you can take a lot of time off from, because the minute you stop posting is the minute you lose that momentum you've built. You have to be consistent, so people think to themselves, *Oh, I'll go and see what so-and-so is doing today, what she's wearing today.*

I try to post on my grid every day. If I miss out on two, three, even four days, it isn't the end of the world. And I like to post in the evening because, personally, that performs better for me (although on a Friday or Saturday I'd probably try to catch people in the morning instead. And if I ever take a two-day break, I would probably do that over the Friday and Saturday).

But even if I'm not posting on my grid, I do try to always post on my Stories, just so people know that I've not disappeared. Sometimes, I find if I take a week off, my followers will say, 'We missed you!' or 'Where are you?' So a break is not necessarily a problem. But after about three days of not posting, I do start to stress a little bit, thinking, *I need to get a picture up!* And if I took too long or did it all the time, I feel like people would say, 'She's not bothered anymore about supplying us with content, so sack her off!' It can feel like pressure to always be posting.

How I deal with that is that I'm always sharing what I'm doing – if it's not necessarily creating an Instagram post for my main feed, I'll be putting up Stories and sharing things that way. I always think influencers that don't make the most of Stories are really missing out, because it's a different way to connect with your audience on Instagram, rather than just showing a highlight reel in terms of that one grid picture a day. You're showing a bit more behind the scenes – it's a little bit like YouTube. So, I'll take photos and video for my Stories as I go about my day: snap a quick picture before I've got to get on a work call, say, that will let people know I'm still alive! I think that's the best way to build a good relationship with your followers: keep your sharing as frequent as possible. There is a reason why so many influencers give the same Instagram advice, which is to stay consistent, upload as much as you can and share as much as you can.

Recently, I've got into a habit of posting photos and videos on my Instagram Stories at the end of the day, rather than as I go: sort of stocking up all my potential Stories for the day and then uploading them all at once. It's partly for security reasons, so people don't know exactly where I am, but also so I can sit down in the evening, sift through what I've taken over the course of the day and decide, *OK*, that *will look good, and then I can post* that. Everything that goes on my social media is carefully orchestrated, but in a natural way at the same time, if that makes sense.

Even when I'm not creating content physically, I'll be thinking about it. Mentally, I'd say 100 per cent of my time is focused on giving people what they want, because it's constantly on my mind. There's never a minute of my day where I'm not thinking about it, because that's my full-time job. And it's definitely taken me a long time to work out what works for my Instagram and try different things to narrow it down. These days, I see my feed as a diary of what I'm wearing, what I'm doing and where I'm at.

HOW I MIX IT UP

One of the defining things about my content is that it's so mixed, visually – my feed doesn't have any theme, colour code or fixed aesthetic. Instead, whatever I want to post, I'll post, which I like because sometimes when a feed looks too perfect, it's not relatable and it doesn't feel like real life. As a user, I like to scroll down a feed and see someone in different places and in different outfits, and for each photo to look different. That's why, if you go on my feed, it's quite colourful and varied. Don't forget, I've been posting for years, so I need to keep it fresh!

I love how effortless it feels to post whatever I want that day – I love it when a feed feels unplanned and easy-going.

I tend to keep my posting style pretty simple. I put together an outfit I love and find a spot to shoot it that feels organic or fits with what I'm doing that day. I think that's why people engage with my content. They like how my posts aren't too perfect or preened; the outfits that I wear are not hard to achieve, the make-up I wear is not hard to do, and the hair isn't either – it's all quite relatable, I feel, and I think that's why I have such a variety of people following me. That young girl can copy my outfits, but maybe her mum or auntie wants to have a look, too.

Another aspect of my Instagram style that has remained constant is that it's never been at-home content. What I mean by that is, some people's photos really perform well when they take them right next to a white wall or in their living room or elsewhere in their house. But mine don't: I always say that my content performs better when I create it while I'm doing the things that I would be doing normally, out and about, like getting a coffee with my boyfriend. For example, I'll post a picture if I'm at the warehouse for Filter by Molly-Mae, so people can see that I'm working, and I post a lot of travel pictures when I'm away. When I've gone away on trips, the photos I took in those places performed really well because they were a little bit different.

People just seem to respond better if I take content while I'm doing different activities, at different locations, and they just don't really like it when I'm at home!

I try to take my Instagram content on days where I'm actually out doing something already. I just feel it's more relatable.

That's partly why I don't really plan my content in advance. A lot of influencers do: there are apps you can use to plan and perfect it all in a grid, so you know how it's going to look. But I find that my followers interact better with me when I'm a bit freer – when I wear whatever I want to that day, and I post it. Plus, I can't work too far in advance because I end up hating the pictures I've taken if I don't post them straight away! So I work to a very short timescale – that just works best for me.

Of course, sometimes there might be a really cool location in Manchester city centre where I want to shoot, or I'll find inspiration for a location on Pinterest or via other influencers. But I always feel that, to my followers, it can be a little bit obvious I've specifically taken the time to go to a location to get a picture. And I like to be original – but not *too* original because people don't want to see anything too different from your usual vibe and theme. Once you've established yourself a bit, they're following you for a reason: because they like what you already post. So, they don't want to see you mix it up *too* much.

CREATING THE PERFECT POST

As for the practicalities, these days, it's two girls called Ellen and Erin, who both work for Fran, who help me with my pictures. They'll come to mine pretty much every weekday and help me with my content. Obviously, I can film an Instagram Story by myself, but if there's a very lengthy brief from a brand for a sponsored Story, then it becomes a two-person job, in terms of making sure that I cover everything in the brief. And in terms of grid posts, you can't really take those kind of photos – glossier, rather than more casual selfies – by yourself!

That's something that I really struggled with when I first moved to Manchester: finding someone to take pictures of me. I was lucky to make a friend at an event who was also an influencer, and we'd sometimes meet up to take pictures of each other, because she didn't have many people in Manchester who could do it for her, either. These days I have Tommy, but of course he's got things to do as well, so I can't always rely on him to take pictures. I'd say he takes 20 per cent of my photos, and the girls 80 per cent. Really, I couldn't do what I do without Ellen and Erin nowadays, because it would be physically impossible.

Not realistic is not relatable!

At the start of every single photo session, I will first take a reference picture of the background, showing what I want it to look like in terms of what to include and what not to include, so that whoever is taking the photos can follow that as a template. That reference picture also lets me check that the background is going to look right with my outfit, that it's not too busy, that the lighting is good. So, at the start of every single photo session, there's always a picture of the background taken without me in it.

Then I just jump in the middle of that, and that's going to be the shot! I'll pull a bit of a stern face – I'm not typically smiling – and start moving, telling whoever's my photographer: 'Just keep tapping away, I'll keep moving, and we'll get the shot.' About every 20 pictures, I'll quickly look through and see if I'm doing the right thing, favourite a few, and get back to it. And I'll keep checking the photos as I go, so that I know what to change or how to stand.

In terms of kit, it's always an iPhone – never a professional camera. If I were ever to use a professional camera to take a picture, the post wouldn't perform well. Again, that's just what I've learned from my time on the platform: not realistic is not relatable. People want to feel they could create a similar image themselves if they had a spare afternoon. If not, they don't engage with it – and they really can tell if I've used a professional camera, even if I'm not in a studio! One year, I launched a collection with photos taken on a professional camera, and it didn't perform quite the way it would if it had been taken on an iPhone. That's why I'm so glad I had built up my audience before I got the exposure of going on a TV show, because it was at that stage where I learned what worked and what didn't. Now, when I've got millions of followers, I don't make those mistakes.

Before I can post the photo, though, I've got to have a caption … and captions, oh my God, are the bane of my life. Honestly, Erin and I have this running joke that I constantly ask her, 'Can you think of a caption?' and we can never think of anything! But I do think that a caption can change how a post performs. If you have a good, witty caption that goes with the photo, I do think it can make people engage with it a bit better. Sometimes I'll scroll down the Explore page, for inspiration, or I'll scroll down my own feed and see what I've used ages ago that maybe I could reword. It all depends on the picture, but it can be a bit frustrating, because you've got the photo already, made sure it looks great, and then you can sit for about an hour thinking about the words!

My overall strategy is to keep it short and sweet, and to go with the aesthetic of the picture. By that I mean I normally just base the caption on what type of picture it is: for example, if it's an outfit-focused picture, then maybe I'll mention something about the pair of shoes I'm wearing. Or, say, if I'm wearing an all-black outfit, I'll refer to that. Or if I'm in a particular city or destination, I might talk about where I am. I don't like to tell a full story in the caption; I think people just want to read something quickly, look at the picture, and then double-tap it and swipe past.

That's what works for *me*. I know some people find that their audience loves to read what they're doing that day in great detail, down to what they've had for breakfast. I've never tried that, but I've noticed before when I've put up a photo relating to a launch with a long caption talking about how much work I put into it and that kind of stuff, people haven't tended to engage with it. And I personally, don't love to read long captions. I think, *I can't be bothered reading that,* and I just scroll past! So, you have to find what works for you and the audience you're building.

And I don't tend to use hashtags anymore. That was the known way to grow your audience, back in the day: you hashtagged the crap out of your picture! Which meant anyone clicking on a hashtag you'd used could find your content that way. But hashtags are not really a thing now in the same way; after all, people can just go to their Explore page instead to find content they'll enjoy.

MY YOUTUBE STRATEGY

YouTube definitely feels like a very separate part of my business, for the simple reason that it takes so much time, especially when you do everything yourself, as I do. Whenever I post a YouTube video, it always feels like a moment of accomplishment for me, after that process of going from nothing to filming a video, editing it and posting it. I love when I get to the end result, I post a video and can pat myself on the back: *Another one up!* I always feel really happy with myself for doing it.

My YouTube channel plays a massive part in building a relationship with my followers. To go on my channel and to actually see things that you don't see on my Instagram means that I'm not just sharing a highlight reel of my life; I'm sharing the behind the scenes, too. I'm showing the good days, but also the not so good days – the days where I've had a breakout on my face as I come on my period, or I've had an argument with my boyfriend. I'm very transparent and real on there, and I think that's why on Instagram – where things might look a bit glossier – people still relate to me well: because they know that not everything is perfect, that not everything is always what it seems. Nothing's a secret on my YouTube, and people know that they'll get the real, raw version of me, who has bad days and good days, which I think makes me more relatable.

And I love YouTube, because it's such a positive platform, and my subscribers are really supportive and uplifting. People come to your YouTube when they're really invested in you, and they care about you as a person. Because why else would you watch a 25-minute vlog of someone's holiday? If you're investing your time in watching a long video of someone's day, you're really only doing that because you want to see what they're up to and hear what they're talking about (unlike other platforms, where it's easier to just 'hit and run'). I honestly would say that for every one negative comment I get on YouTube, there will be about 99 positive ones.

> *YouTube is definitely my favourite platform because I feel like the following is really supportive on there – everyone's so lovely.*

I struggle with it, though, because it is so time-consuming. I've never hired a video editor because I don't feel comfortable with someone having that control over that really vulnerable, uncut side of my life. I like to be able to control completely and utterly what goes out to an audience. Plus, I am a complete perfectionist in terms of what I create and put out! So, while it's time-consuming, I film and edit all my videos myself from scratch.

I don't script them at all. I actually vlog really off the cuff – whatever I'm doing that day, I'll just pick the camera up, film it and talk away. You don't need to worry too much about what you're talking about, either. People absolutely love to just hear you waffle on about your life, and I know that they do because I love it myself – I like YouTube channels where I can really get into someone's life and feel like I know them through their channel. I like hearing the nitty-gritty!

I have loads of favourite YouTubers that I watch: Patricia Bright's still a favourite of mine; CC Clarke (CC Clarke Beauty); Jaclyn Hill; Rachel Leary; Anastasia Kingsnorth. I'll be doing my make-up and put one of their videos on in the background and I'll just feel a bit comforted, like I'm not sat in the room alone.

And I love just flicking through my homepage and watching anything that looks good. YouTube used to be more about sit-down videos, just talking, talking, talking! These days, I prefer watching vlogs – I feel like vlogs are really where the platform has moved on to now. By that I mean more of a fast-paced, day-in-the-life format – where you can really see what someone's up to in their day, where they go, what they do, and where every scene is different. That's what performs best for me these days: vlogs will get my highest engagement compared to sit-down videos. I do love a haul, don't get me wrong, but after you've watched hauls for years, it's understandable that people are all about the next big thing, which right now is vlogs.

I like hearing about somebody else's ups and downs, too; if I'm not having a great week, it's comforting to realise they're going through something similar. Or, if they're having a great week, you get a boost too! You get really invested in someone's else's life through YouTube. That's why YouTubers can experience very high engagement on Instagram, because people know the person behind the picture. So, I always tell my influencer friends – or anyone who wants to be an influencer – to start a YouTube.

LIGHTS, CAMERA, ACTION

In terms of kit, I have a ring light, a little digital camera and a tripod – and that's it, most of the time. Sometimes I'll even just use natural light. For example, when we moved recently, I wasn't able to get my camera and light set up immediately, so I used daylight to film a haul. I had the blinds open in front of me to illuminate my face, and the other blinds shut behind me (you want your light source to be in front of you, rather than lighting you up from behind, which would mean your face is in shadow).

Obviously in the winter it can be more practical to use artificial lighting, because if you're filming a video at three o'clock it'll be pitch-black by four. Likewise, if I film at night, I use three lights: my ring light and two studio lights either side of me. But both natural and artificial light can look good. All my vlogs are filmed using daylight, because obviously I'm not going to carry those lights around with me everywhere if I'm filming in the car or moving around the house.

Sometimes I wonder if I should invest a little bit more in my kit and the rest of it, because I have a lot of people watching my videos, so I should be trying to perfect what I put out. But I feel like if it's not broken, don't fix it. People seem to enjoy my videos as they are – my content isn't too high-res, so again, it could feel unrealistic if I were to up the production standards! The best way to build a relationship with your audience is by being super relatable.

After filming, I edit my footage using iMovie, which comes installed on a MacBook. I've downloaded loads of different software tools before, but I just stick to what I know because I find iMovie super easy. I taught myself how to use it when I was about 15 and now I feel like I could edit a video with my eyes shut! You can watch tutorials on YouTube, but it's that simple to pick up that you could just learn like I did, by importing a video into iMovie and just playing around.

As for what to keep in and cut out, Tommy started a YouTube channel recently and asked me to teach him how to edit. Explaining it to him reminded me that the knack of editing is all about understanding what the audience wants to see – and what they don't. You have to really focus on what your audience is looking for and get rid of whatever they're going to be bored by. Just think, *Well, would I want to see that? Would I want to see someone talk for 30 minutes about that topic … or even five?* That's why it's great to have a passion for watching YouTube if you want to be a YouTuber, because you will automatically start to know what works and what doesn't.

GETTING INTO TIKTOK

TikTok was definitely something out of my comfort zone. It took me a while to be convinced to join because when it first came out, I thought, *No way. I'm not going on that – I don't need another platform to worry about right now. I can barely keep up to date with the ones I've got!* But it's good to try new things, including new apps – after all, that could be where your audience goes next. (And I do feel that TikTok is the up-and-coming platform that could overtake YouTube and Instagram at some point in the future.) So, after a while, as I kept hearing about it, I told myself, *Well, I don't need to take it that seriously,* and finally downloaded it.

I actually made myself understand the app a little bit before I started posting videos on it. I'd watch videos and soon I began to understand what people were posting and talking about. When I actually started to enjoy the app a bit, I began posting myself. I'd always recommend that when you join a new platform: it's so much more natural to learn it as a user and a follower yourself, rather than jumping in and expecting people to follow you on a platform you don't quite get!

I still don't find it the easiest platform to post on. I actually find it quite hard – I don't know how people do these crazy creative videos. I can't do them! I can edit a YouTube video very well, but TikTok, I just can't grasp it. But that's OK: sometimes I'll post really simple, silly videos on there. In the same way I feel Instagram is for my glossier, more polished content, and YouTube is where I'm super real and relatable, TikTok is a place where I can just have fun. You don't have to post the exact same content across every platform. It's much more enjoyable, for you and your followers, if you adapt to each one.

THE TROUBLE WITH TWITTER

I have used Twitter in the past … but Twitter can be a really toxic platform. If you say one wrong thing on Twitter, it's game over for you. People on there like to criticise anything you say, so I've actually deleted the app from my phone now. I used to like to see what people were saying about what I was up to: if we did a Filter by Molly-Mae campaign, for instance, I'd be on Twitter every day, checking the responses to see how it was being received. If someone takes time out of their day to tweet about something, they obviously care about it quite a lot. But while some feedback is helpful, it just started to get so nasty that I deleted the app. My account is still there, but I don't plan to get back on it anytime soon. I just don't think it's a positive platform for me, sadly.

FINDING YOUR NICHE

With so many platforms, it can feel hard to find a place for yourself online – how to do so is my most-asked question from people these days, in different forms: 'How can I grow on Instagram?' 'How can I grow on YouTube?' 'How can I get a following?' To grow these days, it can feel like you have to be doing something so different to everybody else. The influencing industry's grown from nothing into this huge, competitive world.

That's why, if you're keen to get started, I think it's important not to focus on just one platform: TikTok is 'the one' right now – and no doubt there will be the next big thing to explore eventually. But it's really important to be active on all the key platforms. As I said, I didn't actually want to transition to TikTok at first, but I knew that that was where things were heading. More specifically, I'd still say if you're looking to grow a bit of a following on Instagram, start a YouTube channel too, because I do believe that my YouTube is what helped me to create a relationship with my Instagram audience; it complements it really well.

The other thing I always say is that, if you're going to start an Instagram page or any other social feed – and this is a bit of a cliché, because all influencers say it, but it's important – do it because you enjoy it. Not just because you want to make money from it, but because you *actually* enjoy posting your outfits or your travels or whatever it is that you want to share. Because that just takes the pressure off it all a bit, which also helps you stick with it. After all, I didn't earn a penny from Instagram for about three years while I was building up my following. I just did it because I really did enjoy it, and I hoped that in the future something could lead from that.

BUILDING BRAND
MOLLY-MAE

Whatever the platform I'm using, I'm very choosy about what I post and don't post. I know that everything I do is a representation of the brands I work with and, just as importantly, myself – as someone with a public profile and a platform, people respond to me as a brand too, funny as that might sound. I've had to find a balance of living life, but also making sure that everything I do represents me in a way that I want to be seen.

Because that's just so important to me, that everything about me – from what I post, down to the way I come across in meetings – comes across in the right way. I think that in every aspect of life, you have to be the best version of yourself to help you achieve your goals.

*Everything you say and do represents
who you are as a person. And that
applies to whatever stage you're at.*

It's been like that for me from almost the very start: I'm so cautious
about everything I post. Of course, when I look back to when I was
a kid, I was less conscious of what people were thinking – but I have
to care more now because everything I do is scrutinised. And I think
there is also just a natural change that comes with getting older: you
start to care more about what people think and how people perceive
you – and not acting like an idiot in front of certain people!

That doesn't mean I always present the glossiest version of my
life. I try to keep it real. I appreciate my life is not your typical
23-year-old's life. But this is the life I'm living. All I've ever aimed
for in my life is to do things to the highest level I can achieve – and
I think girls have been inspired to believe they can do the same.
Which means a lot to me, I love that.

However, I do make an effort in terms of the energy I project, in
keeping it positive. That doesn't mean I shy away from the negative
– as I've said, I don't try to hide the bad days or arguments with my
boyfriend. But, for example, recently I filmed a vlog introduction
and I opened by saying, 'Oh, I've had a really rubbish few weeks –
I've been really down. I've been having anxiety. I'm stressed out.'
And then I sat on that for an hour and thought, *Nah, I can't start
a vlog like that.* I didn't want people to feel, *God, she's draining the
life out of me!*

So I filmed it again, saying, 'Hey, guys, I've already started this vlog once, but I just want to be a bit more upbeat and later I can talk about what's been going on.' I was still transparent, but I opened it more positively because I think people aren't coming to my channel for the opposite! If you're having a bad week, then yes, you may want to see that I too am having a bad week, and that you're not alone, but you don't want me to drag you down and make you feel worse. It's about being open and honest, but also being that place for people to escape to if they want, so they can come and watch a snippet of your life without it draining them.

I'm all about keeping it real, but also understanding that my job is what I post. I like to keep myself – my brand – consistent and post a similar kind of content, so people know what to expect from me and know that, if they like it, they can come back for more.

WHEN MILLIONS WATCH

If I didn't share the lows or when things went wrong, it might be intimidating and not ring true, because no one has a perfect life – and I certainly don't. As an influencer, I think it's important to share those moments when things don't go your way. I think that's why I have a loyal fan base: because my followers have seen the ups and downs of my journey. As you know, when I've had filler done and it's gone terribly wrong, I've not shied away from explaining that. I'm very transparent when it comes to mistakes I've made or things that maybe I wouldn't do again, because it's a journey and one I want to share.

So, I try to be relatable and say what I want to say. But, over time, I've also learned more about having that control of what I'm putting out there and being careful. Your twenties can be hard years, as you're making so many mistakes. That's so normal because it's an age when you're learning so much. But I'm doing that with millions of people watching me!

When I'm posting out on my platforms I always stop twice and think about what I put out there. If ever I need a second opinion, I will always check with either Fran, my sister or someone else to see what they make of it. I ask them, 'How would you feel watching this Story?' or 'How would you feel reading that caption?' just to check that different people wouldn't find it offensive.

I will check at least a few times with different people before I post something: 'If you didn't know me and saw this on my Instagram, how would it make you feel?'

I always want to know other people's opinions, because I've made mistakes before where in my mind something seemed completely acceptable to post, but other people took it a different way, because of course everyone thinks differently. So, it's just about checking things over: everything I post is a representation of me, and it needs to represent me well.

Still, if you think about having millions of people watching, it's impossible to make sure you're catering for every single person and keeping every single person happy. Everyone has different opinions, and you can't really cater to each person's needs. From having this public platform, I know that whatever I say and whatever I do, there will always be somebody who hates it – that's just the way it is.

HOW I DEAL WITH CONTROVERSY

I've definitely learned about controversy the hard way: by making mistakes – for instance, when the way that I worded something online or said something publicly totally didn't register in my mind the same way that my audience took it. That's happened to me so many times! It has definitely been a learning curve in the last few years. I just don't naturally hold back in what I say, and sometimes I can say too much, or just the wrong thing. I always say I have at least one scandal every few months, when I'll be trending on Twitter. I do my best to avoid it, as the backlash over the next few days is horrible – a terrible, terrible time – depending on what I've done.

At times, I have felt horribly guilty that I've upset people. When I look back, I think, *I shouldn't have said that.* It has really underlined for me that I've just got to triple-check – either in my own mind or with someone around me – how something comes across before I post it or say it. I don't always get it right.

That's why I don't always weigh in when bad things happen in the world. I do try, and I think spreading awareness of certain issues is really important. But it's hard because you're always going to upset someone whatever you say, and sometimes, I'm not knowledgeable enough to speak on a really serious topic. I wouldn't want to share an opinion unless I knew 100 per cent of what I was saying was factual, and educated, because I have a responsibility to my followers.

Even when I talked on YouTube about my endometriosis diagnosis, and some people were really happy that I was talking about something that affected them, there was some backlash that I wasn't speaking about it in enough detail. But I wasn't a doctor or any other type of medical expert – I had just been diagnosed and I was still learning about the condition myself.

Sometimes, when you have a platform, it can feel as if you're expected to always know everything about everything. But I'm just a 23-year-old girl who got plummeted into this new world – it doesn't make me smarter! It doesn't make me more educated on topics. I'm still the exact same as everybody else at this age. I think there's a lot of pressure to always be spreading the right information and be 100 per cent accurate on everything you're saying, which is just impossible for anyone to do if they're busy commenting on everything that happens. It's just not feasible.

But just because I don't comment on something, doesn't mean I'm not interested, or that I don't care – it can be the total opposite.

FOCUSING ON THE POSITIVE

As you'll have gathered, I'm not always the best at dealing with backlash. For a while, I think I focused on the 5 per cent of negativity I would face, more than the positivity. And I don't think I've changed totally in that I do still read what people are saying online – Tommy can't understand why. But because I care so much about my audience and how people are relating to me, I always want to know what people are thinking and how they're responding to me.

But I would say that – as cliché as it sounds – everyone's going to have an opinion, whether you like it or not, and you can't stop people from voicing theirs, no matter how hard you try. For me, understanding and accepting that has meant learning to listen more to the positive comments – because there's more positivity than there is negativity, and I think it's important to focus on and enjoy that. The negative ones, of course, I take on board if someone's pointing out to me in a constructive way that I've got something wrong. I am the first person to say I don't always get it right! But anything else, it just blurs into noise and goes in the category of 'ignore that and move on'. The minute the negativity starts to get to you, that's when you'll crumble.

I have to accept that with every single thing that I post, there will be people that love it and people that hate it – it's literally impossible to cater every post to an audience of 6 million people.

There wasn't a specific moment for me where I realised, *This is where I'll decide to stop caring if people say negative things that aren't fair.* It's been a very gradual process and I'm still not fully there yet: I do still overthink everything I say, everything I post, and I try to keep everybody happy, even though I know it's not possible. But over time, I've definitely got better in terms of starting to be a bit easier on myself and worrying less about what people say.

And maybe I've got a bit more prepared to set the record straight. Fran and I decided a long time ago not to really do many interviews; we've never given many exclusive stories, and we don't work with a lot of press outlets, because we knew there would come a time when I would want to tell my story in my own way and do it in the right way for me, in terms of how people would read about my life and hear what I have to say. When the press writes a story, it's from the journalist's point of view – don't get me wrong, if I gave an interview it could turn out really lovely, but ultimately, the outlet can present it in the way they want to. So, publishing my own book at this stage just fitted in perfectly, because I feel like I've done enough now in my life to really get into what's happened in the last few years and share my journey, and where I'm at now.

I've learned a lot from Tommy too, in terms of how to deal with living a life that people have opinions about. Honestly, nothing fazes Tommy – nothing gets under his skin. It's taken me a while to get to a similar point because when everyone's got their opinion about what you're doing, it's hard not to think, *Oh God is what they say true?*

But I do take inspiration from him when it comes to that side of things because he's really good at handling that – he's got an incredible attitude. He'll say to me, 'Why do you care what they say? You're happy, I'm happy, our families are happy. It just doesn't matter.' He's right. And that genuinely applies to everyone, whether you're trending on Twitter or getting talked about in your hometown. If you and the people you love are happy, don't worry about the haters.

BRANDS AND
BUSINESS

As everyone knows, when you build up a following as an influencer, you can start to work with brands on sponsored content such as Instagram posts and Stories. The way I approach it is to align myself with only a very small number of brands – it just makes more sense to me and to my followers, as I'll explain. So, these days, in terms of working with brands, it really is all about PrettyLittleThing, Beauty Works and Filter by Molly-Mae. They're my main three focuses: PLT and Beauty Works as collaborations, and then Filter by Molly-Mae as my business – my baby!

It all sounds really simple – but that hasn't always been the case …

NOT JUST MONEY MOVES

When people come out of a big show like *Love Island*, they can get blindsided by the money and cheques that are coming forward. But you can't get distracted by things like that – you have to focus on *why* you're doing what you're doing. In my case, I didn't want to come out of the show and only think about making money moves, because as much as I've always wanted to do well for myself, that wouldn't be authentic to me, and I wouldn't stay relatable to my followers. That's why I have had to say no to certain things, to stay true to myself.

Looking back, I'm proud of the way I've always stayed so true to myself. And I've done that because I've had a following for so many years that I've felt so much loyalty towards.

In the first few days after I came out of the villa, about 10 brands came forward and pitched for me to be their brand ambassador, which was so exciting. The deal I accepted in the end was not actually the highest in terms of a number – because I've never been interested in just making as much money as possible. For me, it has always been about making moves that were authentic and building the trust with my followers from the get-go. That's something I've stuck to throughout my career.

I've spoken before about how I once turned down a £2 million deal to be the face of a clothing company. It was crazy!

But I was never going to work with that brand. It didn't represent me. I'd never bought clothes from them before. And I didn't take their deal because I knew it wasn't an authentic move. Even though it was still an incredible brand and one that so many girls would have dreamed to work with, it wasn't the right fit for *my* brand.

When I talked on YouTube about turning down that big deal, so many people reacted – they were shocked. But the truth is, that's something that Fran and I face most days, if not on the same scale: we have potential deals that Fran often won't even put to me because she knows I won't take them. A brand could come to me and offer to pay me however much money, but I still wouldn't take it if I didn't believe in them, because no amount of money is worth me ruining my relationship with my followers.

The moment you take something just for the pay cheque is when you start to become unfaithful to your followers – and I look at my followers as one big family, so I will always be loyal to them. That's something I've always stayed true to: I only showcase clothes I would actually wear and products I actually love. I'd never put my name to something that I didn't completely stand behind, and my followers can trust me in that.

PRETTYLITTLETHING

Of course, when I left *Love Island*, it was PrettyLittleThing that I went with, becoming their new brand ambassador. There was no question that I was going with them, because they had believed in me from day one. They were the brand that really represented me, and always had – that was where my loyalties lay. As I've said, I had a relationship with PLT long before I went on the show, ever since they'd kitted me out with an Ibiza wardrobe when I went out there to work. In another funny twist, their head office is a stone's throw from my very first apartment in Manchester, literally just around the corner.

Collaborating with PLT has really demonstrated to me the value of building a great working relationship over time. Because of this strong partnership, in the summer of 2021, I was announced as the brand's creative director for the UK and EU. That day was insane – an absolute whirlwind. It was hard to take it all in, but it was definitely one of the best days of my life.

My transition to creative director had been in the planning for a good few months. I remember when Fran rang me. I was sat in my car in the driveway. 'Umar's just called me,' she said (that's the owner of PLT), 'and he says he wants you to be the creative director.'

I couldn't believe it. 'Are you joking?'

I was with Maura at the time and told her what the call was about. We're super supportive of each other, so her reaction was just the same as mine: 'Oh my God. That's insane!'

But none of us wanted to get too excited about it at the start, because we knew the deal would be in the works for a while. I knew the brand and what everyone's roles were at PLT: what the buyers did, what the merchandisers did, what the social media team and the creative people did. So, when the role of creative director was raised, I did have quite a good understanding of what that might entail. But obviously, when we got down to the nitty-gritty, there were a lot of discussions about how we would do it, what my exact title would be and what the best course would be to make it all work. There's so much more to getting the right deal done than anyone thinks, so it was a long process. But after many meetings and discussions, we managed to get it over the line.

Then, when we announced my new title, everything went just absolutely crazy. I was trending on Twitter as 'Molly-Mae' and 'Money-Mae' as well – which was ironic because, of course, when I came out of *Love Island*, 'Money-Mae' was trending for all the wrong reasons. But now people were calling me 'Money-Mae' in a positive way – because of the things I've done and achieved. Which really does show how things can turn around!

I made sure to appreciate it all so much, because I knew that in a couple of years' time, I would look back and think, I'd do anything to relive that day again! It was just absolutely huge.

I think the announcement shocked a lot of people, in a good way. Because they knew me as an influencer, for me to become a director within a brand and take on more of a business role was a surprise. Again, it was what I always love: doing something different and outside of the box. That's why it meant so much to me, too: I was really excited to be not just an influencer anymore, and to have more of a business role in a huge brand like that.

The brand is already so current and cool, so I was instantly excited to be able to put my creative spin on things. The role involves working with the marketing, studio, e-commerce and buying teams on campaign launches, product selections and styling. The team are flexible with what I want to do: if I want to go in and spend a full day in the office and go around every department to have a look at what they're doing, the brand activations they're working on, the new campaigns, I can do that. They've really been generous at letting me have a say with anything. So I can take the role wherever I want to take it – and I'm going to work very hard. In fact, there are loads of things I want to do that people probably wouldn't expect. I really have a lot of plans, as you'll see …

BEAUTY WORKS

Beauty Works is a very sentimental collaboration to me. Just like that clothing brand after *Love Island*, a different hair brand offered me a lot of money during that period; but as with PLT, I'd worked with Beauty Works from the start, so I was adamant that I wanted to keep working with them.

It's just such an incredible relationship, and I do really feel that loyalty is something that has given me momentum through the years: that my followers can see I only talk about products that I've used and that I've loved for years.

Beauty Works was the first company that invited me to an influencer event, as I mentioned, and one of the first companies to pay me. I remember Penny, the owner, telling me at that event, 'We just feel you're going to be really big. We have faith in you.' Even when I had 20k followers on Instagram, they were gifting me hair and paying me to do posts. They weren't really working with many girls at that point at all, let alone one with a really small following, so maybe they just saw potential in me – and, of course, that I loved styling hair.

MY HAIR JOURNEY

A lot of influencers struggle with their own hair – some will even have hairdressers come to do their hair and then pretend they've done it themselves! Whereas I was quite lucky in that I had learned how to do it myself, partly because I've always been interested in styling – picking up tips whenever I could by watching YouTube – and partly because of that first job I had at the hairdresser's. Ever since that early YouTube video of me pin-curling my hair blew up, people have been interested to see how I style it (this started long before *Love Island*). And now here I am with my own shade of extensions with Beauty Works! Which just goes to show that even if you can't see it at the time, everything you do can help lead you to where you need to be.

From then on, we started doing posts where I would style my hair with their tools in videos for them. There is one Instagram video that I filmed early on that got millions and millions of views – I'm in a brown top curling my hair at my friend's apartment in Manchester. Beauty Works still use that video now.

I think now that they had been trying for a while to find someone with long hair who could style it quite well, too. And I've always had a passion for hair and was quite good at doing it, which they really liked; they didn't need to give me much guidance with my content – I kind of just took a brief and went where I wanted to with it. So, I felt like I was nobody at the time, but Penny and her husband, Martin, really did back me, which I've always appreciated.

HOW I MADE IT HAPPEN

Every single time I do something bigger with a brand, part of me thinks, *This is where it stops now. Surely this will be the last step a brand wants to take with me!* But then, every time, it doesn't stop: more keeps happening. I've gone from being gifted by these brands, to working with them on a paid level, to being offered deals to be their ambassadors, to now being the creative director of one.

On one level, I know why it's working. If there's one thing I know inside out, it's Instagram. I really understand the platform and so I can really share myself, my style, my life – and the brands that I believe in, which I am so lucky to get to do. I'm loyal, we partner together so well, brands believe in me, and I believe in them. But I also think it's because – despite those anxious moments when I think it's all going to stop! – I believe that things will happen for me, and that I can help make them happen. In the same way I talk about manifesting the reality you want, I do feel that belief – confidence – has helped me tread my own path as an influencer.

My dream was to work with brands in new ways, and together we have achieved that: Beauty Works hasn't had an ambassador partner with them in the way I do before. I've worked with PLT consistently for years now and, at the time of writing, I've put out nine collections with them – which is the most any ambassador has done for the brand.

The consistency in my attitude towards work has never changed. If anything, it has grown stronger: I am more excited about what I do, and what the future could hold, than I've ever been before. I'm not competitive in some things, but with Instagram, I am! Because I've found something I love and which suits me too, I think it's one area where I tell myself, *I will be the best I can at this.*

For me, doing that in a way that has longevity is about always focusing on the bigger picture, and knowing that decisions I make in my career now can really impact my future. I could have taken on so much more work in recent years. But I've always understood that things can be detrimental if you do them incorrectly – taking on too many commitments, or associating yourself with too many brands. That applies to whatever you're doing: establishing longevity is about being knowledgeable when it comes to what's going to accelerate you, and what's going to hold you back.

WHY I LAUNCHED
MY OWN BUSINESS

Soon after coming out of *Love Island*, I started to think about launching my own business. As much as I loved working with other brands – and still do – I already knew that when you have your own business, no one can turn to you and say, 'Actually, we don't want to work with you anymore' because you're the boss!

So, now I love doing both: working with other brands and on my own business. The benefit of the collaborations is that I get to partner with people with different skills or with different experience. And I actually feel that sometimes it's nice that some of the control is taken out of my hands.

When you have your own business, it's not really like that: I'm the boss of my company. Every day, I put as much effort as I can into it, and I'm the person that can decide how far it goes – which also means that the responsibility is entirely on me. And if the day comes that I don't really do Instagram anymore, it's what I'll put all of my effort into.

When Fran and I first talked about the idea of me launching a business, I remember her suggesting make-up. But it just didn't feel like the right avenue for me. I mean, I love make-up, but I'm not particularly good at it! So, I didn't feel strongly enough about make-up to make it my business. But what I did feel passionate about – and what I did feel would work – was fake tan.

And I felt there was a real gap in the market for a new, better fake tan that had a bit of a different price point. There were a lot of cheap fake tans out there, and a lot of really expensive ones, but I felt like that middle price bracket was missing. I'd also heard a lot of people complain about that nasty fake tan smell. So to fill that gap, we created this great formula with a really fresh, bespoke scent. This wasn't something that was already on the shelf to buy; it was something totally new: a tan with a different scent and a different price point. And that's something important to any new business – you need something to differentiate your product from everything else out there.

It wasn't an easy process: we worked for months before putting anything out there. We really worked on hard on getting the bespoke formula right: making sure it was good for people with eczema, making sure it was nourishing, and of course making sure that it smelled good.

Launching Filter by Molly-Mae was a really proud moment for me. I'd watch people reviewing it on YouTube, and they loved the product so much. We've definitely created something a little bit different from the fake tans out there already – that's why, when we recently did a relaunch, everybody came back to buy it – so I feel really proud to have my name on it.

I have such a vision for Filter by Molly-Mae. I really see it being the next go-to tanning brand that you see in all the supermarkets and high-end retailers, and I envision us growing the range of products we offer to take it worldwide. I see myself with my own huge warehouse and beautiful office and a much bigger team. Again, it's my manifesting – I know we'll get there!

In the meantime, I have so much more to do. As with any business, I have to keep investing, both in terms of time and money. I'm still posting everything onto the brand's Instagram myself because I don't trust anyone else to do it – I'm a massive control freak with it, because I'm such a perfectionist! And I don't think everybody realises that: when you're running a business, everything you get is actually plunged straight back into it for the first few years at least. People wait for a long time to make money from a business, knowing that one day it will hopefully repay them, but it's a bet that will take a good few years to come good. So when friends say they want to start their own businesses, I definitely encourage them – and also explain that it's not as easy as people may think! 'Go for it, do it' I tell them, 'but don't do it because you want to get some cash out of it quickly.' Don't get me wrong, I think it's the best thing I've ever done. There are plenty of other ways that you could make a quick bit of cash, and starting a business isn't one of them. It's going to provide for you in years to come, if all goes well – but it's not an overnight thing.

There's so much that goes into a business, it's crazy. But I'm so glad I pushed myself out of my comfort zone to do this, because I've learned so much.

BUSINESS
LESSONS

Being a business owner is something I've had to learn on the job
– and learn quickly! I love being the CEO of my own brand, and
now creative director of another brand; I've always wanted to be a
business-savvy woman. But I can definitely hold my hands up and
say I haven't always been that way!

At first, I didn't have a clue what I was doing. When I first came
out of *Love Island*, I had no understanding of finances or even tax.
On the business side of things, I didn't know about business VAT
and limited companies – I had no idea what they even meant – and
found all this stuff so confusing! Which is fine – most of us don't
learn this stuff in school.

So, starting from scratch, I was very clear with Fran that I needed
to sit down with a financial adviser and have them teach me from
start to finish all the things I just didn't know. Now, I've got a really

great accountant who understands that he needs to explain, in black and white, even what might seem silly things to someone who's already familiar with it all. But it's a new world for me, and that's nothing to be embarrassed about – I've never tried to pretend that I understand something that I don't.

In certain situations – say, if I'm in meetings with important people! – I might not let on that I'm not sure of a detail, but afterwards, I'll just say to Fran, 'OK, so what on earth does that mean? What was that about?' So I play the game – I give the front and then I'll ask questions later! And I'll be honest with the people close to me: 'That bit of the meeting was gobbledygook to me. What did they mean?'

Fran can sometimes tell I don't understand something before I even ask her anything – because I do have this habit of staring off into the distance now and then! If I'm not engaged in something, or I don't understand what's being talked about, I can switch off quite quickly. Over time, I've had to learn how to be engaged and chat back – and, if it doesn't feel like the right moment in the meeting, always make sure to ask the right questions later.

But though I'm young and still learning, I don't feel underestimated. I feel the people I work with are really respectful of me and my team. I'm very lucky in that I've never experienced ageism in that way, or sexism. I've never come out of a meeting and felt, *Cor, they really looked down on me!*

In fact, the only times I've experienced any negativity like that were when I've bought something people might not expect someone like me to be able to afford. Tommy and I always get that from estate agents when we're looking for a house, and when I bought my first expensive watch, I remember the lady working in the shop was so rude to me. When I told her, 'I would actually like to buy this watch,' her attitude changed instantly: 'Oh, OK!'

That was my first big purchase, in fact – a beautiful AP (Audemars Piguet) watch. I had bought my sister a car, and then after that I treated myself to this watch in a shopping mall in Vegas, when Tommy and I were over there to watch Tyson fight Deontay Wilder. It was silver with what they call a factory-fitted diamond bezel – which is a higher finish than when the diamonds are added later. My dad saw the money come out of my bank account and rang me up, not very happy with me! But I was glad I'd treated myself, despite that saleswoman: I planned to keep that watch forever, because it was such a sentimental piece for me, but sadly I wasn't able to (more on that later).

But it's noticeable that at work, I've never experienced anything like that: everyone's been really great. With the brands I work with, it's a two-way relationship that benefits everyone.

Which, if you think about it, goes for any job. Always remember that you've got something to offer, and that respect is the minimum everyone deserves, whatever your age or stage in life.

DODGING THE
COMPARISON TRAP

Of course, it can be hard to feel the best about yourself when you look at where others are at – that's only natural, but it is something to be aware of in case it starts to bring you down.

Starting out, I compared myself a lot to others. At the event to celebrate my current role with PrettyLittleThing, a conversation I had really reminded me of this: my mum and I were talking to Emily Shak, who as you know I really looked up to as a teen. My mum said, 'Emily, you have no idea how many times Molly showed me your Instagram, saying, "I need to be like her, this is what we need to do when we take our pictures."' I definitely used to compare myself to other influencers. I was trying to be like them, and I was trying to get as many followers as they had.

Which is understandable! I think when you're starting out is when you're most likely to compare yourself to others, as you've yet to establish yourself. But in my case, I remember thinking, *God, all these girls are so successful, they're doing so amazingly and I can't even afford my rent!* And that was tough, I really did compare myself. As I've said, it can actually be really helpful to find inspiration in people who are doing what you want to do – but don't let that slide over into you punishing yourself for not being where they are yet.

More recently, I've just really focused on myself – been in my own lane – and I think that has changed a lot for me.

*When you focus on yourself and
don't worry about anyone else,
that's when you really go places.
Comparing yourself never works.*

Of course, that's easier said than done ... so one thing that can help is really focusing on your niche: what *you* have to offer. These days, I actually view myself as no longer solely an influencer, but as a businesswoman, too. So much of my focus is on running my business, Filter by Molly-Mae, and on being creative director of PrettyLittleThing for the UK and EU, that I don't see myself as an influencer alone – although I absolutely still have a passion for it.

Just as when I was starting out on Instagram, I draw so much inspiration from other women: for example, Conna Walker, the owner of House of CB, is so inspiring to me. She's literally conquered the world with her brand – what a woman!

And another huge inspiration would be – of course – Kylie Jenner. I've always said, if I could be anyone for a day, I'd be happy to be Kylie, who has this incredible cosmetics business. Of course, her background definitely meant she had a platform, but she's not just a pretty girl who posts pictures – she's gone and done all this stuff behind the scenes. She has inspired so many girls, including me, to think that we can build our own businesses if we want to.

*I admire anybody that has their
own business – because I know now
what it takes. It's hard work and
so much goes into it.*

So, being a business owner has changed my perspective on who
I compare myself to – and, crucially, I make comparisons in a
positive way. I don't think to myself, *Oh, I wish I was doing that.*
It's more I have a mindset of *Wow, I can't wait for my brand to be
doing that too!* Again, I'm subconsciously manifesting that we'll get
there. And that's always the attitude I've had. I have so many hopes
and dreams for Filter by Molly-Mae – and I feel that's the attitude
you need to have. When you manage your own business, you have
to believe in it wholeheartedly.

HOW I SET GOALS

My main goal these days is just to continue to grow and grow and
grow. I want to grow my business, and keep growing and developing
my partnerships with the brands I work with. At the same time, I
want to keep growing my socials, too – I never want my followers to
subside or just to plateau. I want to keep creating content so that more
people find my page and think, *Oh, who's this girl? I want to follow her!*

And I love the fact that these days, more of my followers follow
me not because I was on *Love Island* but because of the content

that I create. That ultimately gives me so much satisfaction. Still, if I hadn't reached this level by now, I'd actually be appreciative of whatever level of success I'd achieved.

Why? Because I don't necessarily set myself goals by time frames. I think if goals don't happen by the time that you planned, it can be quite disheartening. Now, I just think, *I know we're going to get there – so let's just work towards that.* With Filter by Molly-Mae, for example, it's all about working towards making this brand absolutely huge, but I don't have a set timetable for that.

As with everything in life, I don't like to apply too much pressure – because the minute you start to put pressure on yourself to be better than someone else, or to do better than another business, that's when it starts to get competitive in a bad way. The vibe becomes a bit negative, and it sucks the fun out of it all – which doesn't actually help you work any harder or better to get where you want to be. So, I just try to enjoy the process and take my time, and I know things will happen when they're meant to happen.

You have to work towards your goals gradually, not put too much pressure on yourself.

That doesn't mean you'll always get everything you want. Even when it seems like everything is going your way, there will still be things that just don't go the way you plan. I think people forget that if you're successful; they think your life must be perfect. The reality is, whatever stage you're at, you'll still face let-downs or failures – they just might come in a different way or in a different form to when you were at an earlier stage. But I really do believe that everything happens for a reason.

Recently, I was in talks for a job that I was so excited about – we had hair and make-up planned; we were ready to go. Then I learned they didn't want me anymore. I was heartbroken. But then, a week later, I secured one of my biggest campaigns to date with Starbucks, a brand that I'd always wanted to work with. If the other job had happened, I would have struggled to get the Starbucks one that I really wanted to do. So, I really believe that everything unfolds the way it's meant to. Trust that process – and trust the timing of everything in your life.

Because I do feel like it all works out in the end. So, when things don't go my way, I think, *That's just happened because something else has come in instead*, or *This has got to happen so* that *can happen*. I just believe that all the events in your life are meant to happen in whatever order they take, so that other things can fall into place. I've always thought of it that way, and that's a way of thinking that helps me on my not-so-good days.

ENJOY THE JOURNEY

And when you do reach a goal? Appreciate it!

That's something that I'm still learning to do. I've always been focused on the future, and what I wanted to achieve next. It's a good attitude to have in that it keeps me motivated and working hard; but equally, there is a downside – or at least an aspect to be aware of – because sometimes it means you don't appreciate what you have in the moment.

Looking back, I have struggled with that. For a lot of my younger life, I didn't necessarily enjoy the moment I was in. Having an older sister is probably why, every single year of my life, at every single stage I was at, I always thought to myself, *I wish I was old enough to do this*, or *I wish I was old enough to do that!* At 15 and 16, I remember thinking, *This is rubbish, I want to be older, I want to be able to go to clubs on my own, without having to borrow Zoe's ID!* Then, when you get the chance to do those things, you think, *I don't like doing that ... I want to be* this *age so I can go and do that.* I look back now at trips I went on when I was starting out as an influencer, and think, *Oh my God, I'd love to do that again.* As with everything, though, you don't really cherish it until it's gone.

Now, I would tell my younger self to slow down and stop trying to rush things – and, even when I was 15, just to look at the things I've achieved, at school and in my activities! I'd tell myself, 'Just be proud of that for a minute. Don't be worried about what's coming next, don't be worried about what's the best college to go to, don't be worried about what's going to get people talking – just appreciate where you're at.'

Know that what comes next will come when it's meant to come. Don't get me wrong, it's great to have ambition and drive – I'm all about that! – but stop *worrying* about what you don't have or aren't doing yet. Make sure you enjoy the stage you're at, and trust in the timing of your life.

Wherever you're at, it's important to appreciate that without looking to the future all the time – to be in the moment.

That's something I've really been working on myself: to remember that sometimes I just need to sit down and tell myself, 'You've actually achieved a lot – you've become successful.' That's why, on the day we announced my PLT role, one of the biggest days of my career, I actually took some time to sit in my hotel bedroom by myself to reflect. I even went to the gym at lunchtime, so I could walk on the treadmill with my headphones in, listening to empowering music! I told myself, 'Appreciate where you are right now – because this moment is not going to come again. In two years' time if things have quieted down or you're having a down day, you're gonna wish you were back in this moment.'

So, I'm definitely taking more time out of my days now to recognise and appreciate where I'm at – and I really do think everyone can benefit from doing the same.

FINDING MOTIVATION

What gets me up in the morning is picturing my future and where I know I want to be. Where I am now, I wouldn't even say I'm anywhere near the point that I want to reach. Although, that doesn't mean I see myself stopping when I get there: I work because I absolutely love it!

Recently, my nail tech Corrine did my nails and I quickly posted a picture of them on Instagram. 'Don't you get sick and tired of that?' she asked me. I told her no. I've never felt tired of posting on Instagram, it's a passion for me. It's never been a chore – I do it because I genuinely love posting content. Even if I didn't earn money from it, even if I had another job, I'd still post on Instagram. I love it.

While I really am trying to appreciate the present more, one of the things that still excites me the most in life is just the thought of what lies ahead. I want to do as much as I can and be the best version of myself that I can be. In my professional life, I envision that as I continue to grow on my platforms, and I plan on growing all my businesses. In the process, I will continue to work and work and work. I won't stop until I can provide for my family for years to come, and until I've inspired so many girls to do what they want, too.

And if that isn't the sort of life that you want to have – if you want to do something totally different? Whatever you want to do, great! But I do think that whatever you're doing, it's not OK to hate it. Some of my friends feel that way about their jobs, and I always say to them, 'If you don't love it, you need to leave when you can, because you only have one life and it's not that long.' And I feel that you cannot waste your days doing something that you don't enjoy; you cannot waste your days waking up in the morning and dreading going to work!

We spend so much time in work,
so you have to love what you do.
Aim to be happy!

Because imagine being old in your rocking chair, and looking back and thinking, *God, I wasted 10 years at a job that I hated when I could have been into something that I love.* Now, I'm not saying to just quit your job instantly – I've stayed in jobs I didn't like. We all need money to live, and we all have tough days at work even when we're doing what we want to do. But I think it's important you don't feel you need to remain stuck forever in a place where you don't want to be.

Of course, not everyone has the same background or the same opportunities. And some people start off with a lot more obstacles in their way. So, when good things do happen for you, hopefully, someday, you can help make them happen for other people too – as I really want to do.

PRACTISING
SELF-CARE

DOWNTIME

Don't get me wrong – even when you love what you do, you still need downtime to relax and recharge. Some days, I'll definitely get up and really not feel up to creating content. Sometimes I wake up and just want to put a tracksuit on and not do anything – not have to be that chatty, pristine girl that people expect me to be. Which is fine! So, I definitely take days off – 100 per cent.

DREAM DAYS OFF

On a perfect day off, I could sleep in forever. Yes, it's changed a bit now since moving out of the city centre and getting into a healthier lifestyle, but I can sleep in till around ten or eleven o'clock if I need to! And then I get up, have breakfast and watch TV. I usually go to the gym on my days off as well, because I really enjoy exercise at the moment. It's become a key part of my weekly routine and helps me with everything, mentally and physically. But apart from that, I'll just be sitting on the sofa wearing no make-up whatsoever and watching a film – that's how I really enjoy my days off! I just chill at home, have a bath – baths are just my favourite thing in the world.

In the evening Tommy and I would go on a date: our favourite thing is to go to the cinema and watch a horror film – we're horror-film obsessed. Afterwards, we'd go to dinner; he loves burgers, so we might go to a burger place, or a Pizza Express – anywhere, though we're both normally trying to eat healthy! That's a perfect little evening for us – we don't dress up. I don't wear make-up. And we just have the nicest time. To grab a really posh, fancy dinner and get dressed up – that's not our style at all. We just love a really chilled evening.

At the weekends, whenever we've got free time together, Tommy and I will find something to do that will get us out of the house rather than staying in. We love going on walks – on a Saturday we sometimes go to a park near us for a walk and to see the deer. We love going to the Trafford Centre and just wandering round there, and at Halloween, we'll always go to different Halloween parks – we're always really active.

On a Sunday, if I'm cooking, I'll make a Sunday roast. I went through a stage in lockdown of making Sunday roast every single weekend! I'm not that good at cooking, as a lot of people know, but I've definitely tried to get better. So far I've mastered a roast, but I need to practise a few more recipes because we don't really eat in that much. If we're eating in, it's normally meal preps – because Tommy's always eating clean for his boxing – so we don't cook those from scratch.

MY HAPPY HOUR

If ever people were wondering who the Molly-Mae is that nobody sees … the answer is it's the Molly-Mae that you do see, because of my YouTube! I'm so honest on there and it's such an insight into how I live my life. That's why, at the party to celebrate my current role with PLT, at least three girls came up to me and said the same thing: 'We know that you'd rather be on the sofa with the candles lit watching Harry Potter. We love that we get to have you just one night.'

It was just really sweet. Because I thought, *Oh my God, my followers actually know me so well!* Although, that party was one I had no problem sacrificing my Harry Potter and PJs for. The whole night was an amazing celebration and one I will always remember.

It's just that, at the end of the day, when everything is spotless and I've got a nice cup of tea, that truly is my happiest time of day! I'll usually drink peppermint tea – I drink it by the gallon when it gets to the colder months. I actually only really drink tea when the seasons change, so that's another reason why my favourite time of the year is autumn. I'll have loads of baths and curl up in nice blankets. That's just when I am at my happiest, that time of year. But whatever the season, I'm in my element when I've got the candles on at home and a nice film on the TV and I've had a long bath.

The small things really do give me pleasure – even getting a nice cold bottle of water from the fridge can make me so happy.

LEARNING TO SWITCH OFF

What I do is not a traditional nine-to-five where you go to work, you switch on, and you come out of work and switch off – and I know a lot of jobs aren't like that either, these days. I'm almost constantly switched on because my phone is my job and it's by my side every second. It might sound ridiculous, but it's how I work, it's how I communicate with my followers – it's like my office! And of course with my family four hours away, it's my way of keeping in touch, too.

Zoe and I, in particular, are always on FaceTime with each other – but my friends always laugh about those FaceTime calls because it can just be 'Hi', 'Hi', 'You alright?' We check in with each other and then hang up again! So it might seem short and a bit meaningless, but I like it. I don't always want to be on my phone when I don't have to be. Sometimes when I get a text, I think, *Oh, I'll reply to that later … I can't be bothered to be on my phone right now!*

All that means I do have a habit of being on my phone too much, like a lot of people. Tommy and I actually had a really nice time not so long ago which reminded me of that. We went to Bath for a couple of days and unintentionally I just didn't go on my phone for, really, the first time ever. I had brought all these nice outfits and make-up, but we literally just slobbed out and I wore the same tracksuit and no make-up for three days. I went a bit MIA, and it was lovely.

On another trip, Tommy and I went camping up a mountain in the Lake District with Zoe and her boyfriend – they're both in the army and do things like that all the time, so I rang her to say, 'I really want to do that, too!' Tommy was excited to come as well.

I wanted to do something a bit challenging in that way – sleeping in a tent on the side of a mountain! – because I grew up doing things like that. Not a lot of people know that side of me. I feel like a lot of the time people look at me and just see a girly girl, but as you know now, I grew up going on walking holidays. I'd hate people thinking that I'm this prim and proper girl who wants to have everything done for me. I'm much more hands-on than that. I don't *need* those fancy holidays in five-star hotels. I don't need a big fancy apartment. I like the nice things in life – but I don't need them. And sometimes I enjoy getting away from it all up a mountain!

It was completely different to my usual holidays. We walked really far and pitched our tents out in the open. Which was a little bit scary at times, because at night it was pitch-black on the mountain and you could literally hear a pin drop ... or a stranger's footsteps. It was just after we'd said we were going to sleep when I heard footsteps in the grass, so distinctively. *Oh God!* I thought. But I just told myself,

No, no you're hearing things, just ignore it. Still, the next day, I asked, 'Did anyone else hear footsteps around eleven o'clock?' And we all had … Everyone said, 'I didn't say anything because I didn't want to scare anybody.' I think it must have been a sheep we heard because it was just not possible for anybody else to be up there – we were in the middle of nowhere and didn't see a soul the whole time.

I also didn't have signal literally from the minute I got up the mountain to the second I came down the next day. At first I wasn't keen on being cut off, because obviously, I'm a control freak with my socials, and that stressed me out. But the camping itself was really nice. It was something so different for me and Tommy. Being in the army, my sister and her boyfriend are both super good with compasses and maps, and we felt very safe in their hands. We would never have been able to do it by ourselves – it was proper wilderness camping, and we didn't have the first clue where to start with anything, even setting up the tents! That was all them, so we can't take credit for that. But it was a really good experience.

Straight after that trip, I thought, *I won't be in a rush to sleep on a mountain again anytime soon.* But now, looking back, I think, actually, I probably would like to do that again. It was so nice to do something a bit different, a really, really nice escape. I love that camping was something I used to hate when I did it growing up, but now I choose to do something like that.

So, I think doing things like that – just taking the time to not go on my phone too much or to have a couple of days off Instagram and not worry about it – is so important. As I've said, you do need to build momentum online, especially when you're starting out and trying to actually build some in the first place! But once you've built that relationship with your followers, it doesn't disappear overnight – and that's what I'm trying to remember as my days get busier.

And it's not just about getting away. At the end of the day, when we get to bed, Tommy and I will always pop on a film and make sure to put our phones down. That's something that we love doing at night – finding a new horror film (I'll skip Harry Potter for once!) and watching that together, totally unplugged.

GETTING DEEP

Taking time out is also important for staying on an even keel in terms of how you're feeling. When things aren't going my way, I feel that I know what I need to do in terms of taking a moment to manage my emotions. I've generally been pretty fortunate with my mental health. Even before – before I had my career and my relationship and my home – in tough times, like when I was going through my parents' divorce, I would be quite good at moving on from a bad day. And I'm so lucky to be where I am in my life that now, when I feel a bit stressed or that things are getting a bit on top of me, I can take a breath and tell myself, 'You really have nothing to be stressed about. Just look at what you have and try to put everything into perspective. Sit back, Molly – everything's fine!'

But then there are times when you can't help but be hit hard by a setback. For me, having my home broken into, and having the things I'd worked hard for stolen, was one of those really difficult times and setbacks.

HOW I DEALT WITH THE BREAK-IN

On Thursday, 21 October 2021, I was in London with Tommy and Fran for a Beauty Works event. As a lot of people know, we were broken into that night.

The next day, I was at The Londoner Hotel with Fran at a PLT meeting, when Fran got a call from someone who works with us. She just told me, 'We need to go – your house has been robbed.' I started crying because I didn't know what they'd taken. But even then, the only thing I really cared about was the fact that I had Ellie Belly with me. They could take whatever the hell they wanted; the only thing that was irreplaceable was Ellie Belly!

By the time we got back from London, the police had already been to the apartment to investigate. It was ice-cold as the balcony doors had been left open all night. Tommy and I didn't stay another night there: we moved into Fran's straight away and took everything that was left, just in case the burglars came back.

They took a lot, though. We imagined they'd been in the apartment for hours.

Since both my parents are ex-police officers, they were really vigilant in terms of making sure the police were doing their job correctly and asking the right questions – my dad, in particular. He'll always be a police officer at heart, my dad! As I work on this book, I don't think the police will find them and I don't think we'll ever see the things that they took again. It's heartbreaking to know someone has been in your home and taken what you've worked hard for.

What hurt me the most is that they took things that were sentimental to me. Things that I would love to hand down if I ever had a daughter. But most of the things they took were replaceable and we were safe. Even our stuffed toys, which were what I cared about most, were untouched. They pulled off all the bedding and flipped the mattress, but left all the teddies that were on the bed.

Thank God we had insurance. Fran has always been very on it with that, whereas when I would buy something expensive, I always had the view of *Why should I have to pay more money to insure it?* But now I always tell my friends, you *have* to spend money on insurance. Because when things like this happen, you'll be so grateful that you did. The break-in was something I always worried would happen. When you live your life in the spotlight, it's always something you worry about happening, and I was quite fearful of it because where we lived was on quite a busy road and so many people knew we were there.

In the aftermath of it all, Tommy had to fly to America and start training for a fight, so I had to go to viewings and find a new place on my own. No one knows where it is because now we're really careful – we don't take any chances. It was a really hard lesson for us to learn, but I think it was good to learn. For a couple of weeks after the robbery, I even had round-the-clock security, a close-protection guy who came with me whenever I left the house – which I absolutely hated. Fran wanted me to have it permanently, but I didn't think it was necessary. However, we have stepped up our security, including how we post on social media. Still, it could have happened even if we weren't in the spotlight – these days, if you live in a nice home or you have a nice watch, you can be a target.

MORE THAN MATERIAL

Especially since the burglary, I've felt even more conscious that life really isn't about having designer bags, or anything like that. (It's just about a logo on a bag, at the end of the day!) I do really appreciate how lucky I am to have the things I do now, as it's not always been that way for me. As I said, I never had anything designer when I was younger – when my friends were wearing more expensive labels, I wasn't allowed those sorts of clothes. I was raised very much to understand that those things were not the be-all and end-all.

That doesn't mean I don't enjoy things like that – but I'm also totally fine not having them. Deep down, I'm just a 23-year-old girl who's not yet used to how much my life has changed in the last few years! So every time I've bought something for myself, I've thought, *Oh my God, I cannot believe I actually get to buy this myself now.* When I was younger, I actually thought that the only way I was ever going to have really nice things would be if somebody else bought them for me. When you do it yourself it just tastes all the sweeter – it's so much better.

To have that freedom to treat myself, and to treat my friends too, has been amazing. As soon as I was able to, I bought my sister her car, and I am lucky enough to be able to buy my friends designer bags for their birthdays. I've never done it for any sort of gratitude, I just enjoy it: I spoil them because it's something I've always dreamed of being able to do.

Still, I have always known that it's not just about how much you spend. When Fran had an operation recently, I really wanted to get her something that meant a lot to her. So, I went round Tesco, picking up all her favourite things, from chocolate bars to mugs to notepads to the fabric conditioner she likes, even to the issue of *Cosmopolitan* that we'd worked on together – all our happy memories. I honestly think she liked the thought that had gone into it more than anything else.

So, I would never want anyone to feel that the way to happiness is about what you have. (And no one should *ever* feel that you have to have these things to build a following online – I definitely didn't!)

BOUNCING BACK

I've come to terms with the burglary now. To be honest, if someone told me that I was going to get robbed, I'd have thought it would affect me really badly. But I've moved on from it already. I have realised that, when something bad happens, I'll just deal with it in the moment. I'm not someone who doesn't show their emotions, then they come back to hit them five years on – I just cry about it at the time and then do my best to get over it. Everyone deals with things in their own way, though, and that's also fine!

For me, whatever the situation, the key thing has always been dealing with how I feel there and then. I might go to the gym or just have some time to myself in another way, but the main thing is that I am quite a proactive person: if I have a problem, I'm not going to put it to the back of my mind and let it sizzle away. I try to put it to bed so that I can move on.

I can be quite methodical about it! A friend of mine was actually going through a hard time recently, so I sat with her and wrote out a massive list of all the things that I would do if I were in her position, to help her deal with everything that she was facing. A list really helps me think in terms of *OK, I could try that. If that doesn't work, I'll try the next thing on the list. And if that doesn't work* … and so on. In other words, it helps me come up with a plan of action. And, obvious as it might sound, if you're feeling stuck or unhappy, thinking about what *specific* actions you can take right now to address your situation might help get you out of it – or, at least in the short term, feel a bit more hopeful about the future.

What those actions might be all depends on the situation – it could be boys, it could be work, it could be anything. (And if it *is* a situation with a guy, as it was for my friend, I always say, maybe take a step back and allow the guy to show you how he feels. If you step back and they don't really care, then at least that shows you their true colours; and if they do step up, great.)

That doesn't mean that I walk away when things get tough – I'm always a person to really work at things and persevere before

I give up on them. In times of crisis, I tend to write a long list of ways to salvage a situation or a relationship. And then at the end of it, if none of those things have worked, then I would think about ending it.

Lastly, I think taking control over a situation always helps – showing your authority and that you're not scared to stick up for yourself. I might not like conflict, but I will make clear that I am not a doormat. I always feel that the minute you show a guy – or anybody! – that you'll be walked over and that you're a bit of a pushover, then you're at a real disadvantage.

WHEN YOU CAN'T FIX IT ALONE

All that said, I think it's really important to seek help if you need it – you don't have to try to sort out everything yourself. Recently, I actually started speaking to a therapist, just because I've been dealing with anxiety and it's been quite hard. It wasn't that I felt I couldn't speak to the people around me, who are so lovely and will listen to anything I need to talk about. It's that I didn't want to be constantly talking to them about the same thing that was going on in my mind. So, I started speaking to someone once a week, someone very impartial that I could just talk to about how I'm feeling, and that's been helpful.

I have a very overactive mind – when I get into bed at night, it's going 1,000 miles an hour – and I can think the worst of every situation. But my therapist has helped me talk through and rationalise my anxieties, to help me understand that a lot of the things I might worry about are not actually facts. They're just thoughts. I began to realise that what was on my mind was my imagination running wild with me, rather than the reality of my situation. Talking to her has helped me understand I don't need to catastrophise everything – she's been really impactful for me and my thoughts.

I started seeing her in the run-up to a big fight Tommy had planned, which is one particular reason why I was dealing with a lot of anxiety at the time. Competitive sport terrifies me a little bit: I used to get that nervous stomach ache before competing in sports, or even before a swimming lesson – I didn't like it. Now, I'm transported back into that world because of my boyfriend's profession, and I find it quite hard to deal with the nerves running up to a fight, and looking after him and making sure that I'm supporting him in the best way possible, while also keeping my work life in order.

For this fight in particular, though, Tommy wasn't well towards the end and nobody knew apart from me and his team, so I was keeping this a secret during his whole camp. He had a terrible chest infection and I was trying to nurse him every night. When you love someone, it's almost like you feel what they're feeling, and I just knew how frustrated he was getting that his health wasn't coming back, although he was doing everything he possibly could. Then, after the chest infection, one of his ribs broke because he was weaker than usual and he was still training. It was just horrendous, the whole thing. And with it being such a huge fight – which came with a lot of trash talk – it was a lot for me to handle. It all came at quite a stressful time for me anyway, because of the break-in and what was going on with my health. It was everything at once – a bit of a rough couple of months, really.

I knew that I would go back to my normal self and I'd feel fine again, but something like that can take a massive toll on you. I've definitely understood how much anxiety can affect you day-to-day and how much it can make you lose your focus so that you can't really think about anything else: it really consumes you. That's why I think it's good to speak to someone about it if you can. I'm really lucky to have access to a therapist, but your confidant doesn't have to be a professional. You could also turn to a family member or a friend. At the end of the day, just talking to someone can be enough to lift that burden from your shoulders.

HOPE FOR THE FUTURE

I'm someone who's focused on what is going to bring me happiness. Part of that, for me, is working towards my success, because it means I wake up every day and get excited about what the future holds. And I do feel that having that motivation – that get-up-and-go and that drive to achieve more – can be a key to happiness in other people, too.

Rather than sitting back and looking where you are and thinking, I've not done much with my life, wherever you are at the moment, try to look to the future and think about all the amazing things to come.

Sometimes, I admit, I will just sit on the sofa and think about all the exciting things that I have to look forward to – like Filter by Molly-Mae booming in the way I envision – but they're not always work-related! Being lucky enough to have babies one day – the thought of that makes me so happy and excited. Whenever I'm having a down day, I'll think about that – *Oh my God, imagine that day* – or think about the day I get engaged.

Since meeting Tommy, I have realised how much I can't wait to be a mum. And I know I'm only young, and I always wanted to be that person who had babies when I was past 30 – I wanted to live my life first – but I do think we'd make really, really great parents together if that were to happen for us. I don't want to rush it because I know how important it is to enjoy each stage of life. It's something amazing I can look forward to, so I tell myself, 'Just wait. Just wait!' For now, we've just got kittens – Eggy and Bread (sums me up, really)! But I definitely see us starting a family within the next few years. It's a chapter we're really excited for.

EPILOGUE

AN EXTRAORDINARY LIFE
... FOR YOU TOO

My life now feels a million miles away from my life grow-ing up, but looking back I always knew this was what I wanted. From the early days of fashion school and building my Instagram following, being my own boss as a teenager and moving to Manchester on my own, I found a confidence in myself that I hope is helpful for other young girls to read about. On one level, I still can't quite believe it. How did this happen? My dreams actually came true – it's just mad!

I think it's about finding that balance. It's important to be happy where you are, to appreciate each stage you're at and trust the process. But never lose that drive to keep chasing your dreams. That's something I always tell people.

Looking back, my life unfolded really quickly – and I feel like everything happened for a reason. By that I mean every job, every small thing, had something to teach me. It's funny how these things work. So, if you have a tough day, if something bad happens, remem-ber that that's not the end of the story.

You will make mistakes in the process – I certainly have – and that's OK. At the same time, I know it sounds cliché, but I literally wouldn't change anything that's happened. You have to make mistakes so that, later on in life, you won't repeat them, and you can share the lessons you've learned, so that others won't make the same ones either.

The one last thing I want to say – and these are words I so firmly believe and live by – is that you only have one life, so you have to *live* it. If you take anything away from my story, please make it that! If you wake up one day and think, *I want to do this*, go and try it. Even if it's just a little thing, even if you just want to learn a new hobby, do it!

One of my biggest fears is that I'll look back later in life and think, *I wish I tried that.* I want to give *everything* my best shot so that one day, when I'm old, I can finally tell my grandkids, 'I tried everything that I wanted to do. I made mistakes – but I don't have any regrets.'

I know how lucky I am to be able to share 'My Story' with you. Especially as it's a story I'm still writing. In fact, this is only the first chapter. I can't wait to see what else there is to come!

ACKNOWLEDGEMENTS

First and foremost, thank you to my family: Mum, Dad and Zoe. I am who I am today because of you guys. Thank you for everything you have done and continue to do for me every day to guide and support me in everything I do.

Tommy, I couldn't wish for a better boyfriend. Thank you for being my number one always and being by my side no matter what. They don't make them like you anymore. I am proud to say you're mine.

To Fran, my manager, Erin and Ellen, thank you for making everything we do possible. I couldn't wish for a better team.

I want to thank every single supporter, subscriber and fan, and all of my followers. I want to thank you all for your loyalty and being with me on this journey. Thank you to every single one of you. Without you guys I wouldn't be anywhere.

Thank you to Lydia and the team at Ebury for giving me the opportunity to share my story so far. Thank you to Emma for helping me put all my thoughts into words so perfectly.

To all the incredible brands I get to work with every day and along the way, thank you. Every opportunity has led me to today and I am so grateful for every job I have done. To PrettyLittleThing, thank you for believing in me and letting me share my vision with you. To the BeautyWorks team, thank you for being with me since the very start. You have supported me more than you will ever know.

… and to all of you reading this book, thank you! This is just the start.

P.S. Can't forget to thank Ellie Belly for being with me through absolutely everything. Life wouldn't be the same without you every step of this journey. Every memory I have experienced with you.